Law: A Very Short Introduction

VERY SHORT INTRODUCTIONS are for anyone wanting a stimulating and accessible way in to a new subject. They are written by experts, and have been published in more than 25 languages worldwide.

The series began in 1995, and now represents a wide variety of topics in history, philosophy, religion, science, and the humanities. Over the next few years it will grow to a library of around 200 volumes – a Very Short Introduction to everything from ancient Egypt and Indian philosophy to conceptual art and cosmology.

Very Short Introductions available now:

AFRICAN HISTORY
  John Parker and Richard Rathbone
AMERICAN POLITICAL PARTIES
  AND ELECTIONS L. Sandy Maisel
THE AMERICAN PRESIDENCY
  Charles O. Jones
ANARCHISM Colin Ward
ANCIENT EGYPT Ian Shaw
ANCIENT PHILOSOPHY Julia Annas
ANCIENT WARFARE
  Harry Sidebottom
ANGLICANISM Mark Chapman
THE ANGLO-SAXON AGE John Blair
ANIMAL RIGHTS David DeGrazia
ANTISEMITISM Steven Beller
ARCHAEOLOGY Paul Bahn
ARCHITECTURE Andrew Ballantyne
ARISTOTLE Jonathan Barnes
ART HISTORY Dana Arnold
ART THEORY Cynthia Freeland
THE HISTORY OF ASTRONOMY
  Michael Hoskin
ATHEISM Julian Baggini
AUGUSTINE Henry Chadwick
BARTHES Jonathan Culler
BESTSELLERS John Sutherland
THE BIBLE John Riches
THE BRAIN Michael O'Shea
BRITISH POLITICS Anthony Wright
BUDDHA Michael Carrithers
BUDDHISM Damien Keown
BUDDHIST ETHICS Damien Keown
CAPITALISM James Fulcher
THE CELTS Barry Cunliffe

CHAOS Leonard Smith
CHOICE THEORY Michael Allingham
CHRISTIAN ART Beth Williamson
CHRISTIANITY Linda Woodhead
CLASSICS
  Mary Beard and John Henderson
CLASSICAL MYTHOLOGY
  Helen Morales
CLAUSEWITZ Michael Howard
THE COLD WAR Robert McMahon
CONSCIOUSNESS Susan Blackmore
CONTEMPORARY ART
  Julian Stallabrass
CONTINENTAL PHILOSOPHY
  Simon Critchley
COSMOLOGY Peter Coles
THE CRUSADES Christopher Tyerman
CRYPTOGRAPHY
  Fred Piper and Sean Murphy
DADA AND SURREALISM
  David Hopkins
DARWIN Jonathan Howard
THE DEAD SEA SCROLLS Timothy Lim
DEMOCRACY Bernard Crick
DESCARTES Tom Sorell
DESIGN John Heskett
DINOSAURS David Norman
DOCUMENTARY FILM
  Patricia Aufderheide
DREAMING J. Allan Hobson
DRUGS Leslie Iversen
THE EARTH Martin Redfern
ECONOMICS Partha Dasgupta
EGYPTIAN MYTH Geraldine Pinch

Available soon:

For more information visit our website
www.oup.com/uk/vsi
www.oup.com/us

Raymond Wacks

LAW

A Very Short Introduction

OXFORD
UNIVERSITY PRESS

OXFORD

UNIVERSITY PRESS

Great Clarendon Street, Oxford OX2 6DP

Oxford University Press is a department of the University of Oxford.
It furthers the University's objective of excellence in research, scholarship,
and education by publishing worldwide in

Oxford New York

Auckland Cape Town Dar es Salaam Hong Kong Karachi
Kuala Lumpur Madrid Melbourne Mexico City Nairobi
New Delhi Shanghai Taipei Toronto

With offices in

Argentina Austria Brazil Chile Czech Republic France Greece
Guatemala Hungary Italy Japan Poland Portugal Singapore
South Korea Switzerland Thailand Turkey Ukraine Vietnam

Oxford is a registered trade mark of Oxford University Press
in the UK and in certain other countries

Published in the United States
by Oxford University Press Inc., New York

© Raymond Wacks 2008

British Library Cataloguing in Publication Data

Data available

Library of Congress Cataloging in Publication Data

Data available

ISBN 978-0-19-921496-9

1 3 5 7 9 10 8 6 4 2

Typeset by SPI Publisher Services, Pondicherry, India
Printed in Great Britain by
Ashford Colour Press Ltd, Gosport, Hampshire

Contents

Preface

Seldom do the words 'law' and 'brevity' occur in the same
sentence. The notorious prolixity and obscurity of the law may
suggest that any attempt to condense even its rudiments is
an undertaking of Utopian, if not quixotic, proportions. But
this is the improbable task I have undertaken in these pages:
to distil the essentials of the complex phenomenon of law: its
roots, its branches, its purpose, practice, institutions, and its
future. My objective is to introduce the lay reader – including
the prospective or novice student of law, politics, or other social
sciences – to the fundamentals of law and legal systems, avoiding
as much technical jargon as possible. I hope that this little
volume will encourage curiosity about the intriguing nature of
law, and promote further reflection upon and exploration into
the central role it plays in our lives. Those in search of a deeper
understanding of the numerous facets of the law will want to turn
to some of the works listed in the 'further reading' section. There
is also, of course, an abundance of excellent online legal resources;
some of the leading websites are provided in Chapter 6.

It is important to stress that, though the emphasis of the book is
on the Western secular legal tradition (the common law and the
civil law), I include brief discussions of other legal systems, such
as Islamic law, customary law, and certain mixed systems, since
my principal purpose is to offer an introduction to 'law' in its most

general sense. I confess, however, my predisposition towards the common law. This prejudice, if it is to be so described, might be defended by pointing to what I see as a perceptible shift towards the globalization of various features of the common law. But that is too glib a rationalization. The explanation is less oblique. English is the language in which this book is written by one who has spent most of his working life in common law jurisdictions. My limited proficiency in foreign languages dictated that all the sources, including those related to non-common law systems, were in English. Despite this encumbrance, I have attempted to curtail any gratuitous assumptions about the law that may spring from my own experience which, as it happens, is unusually diverse. I studied and taught law in a mixed legal system (South Africa) as well as in two common law jurisdictions (England and Hong Kong), and I now live in a civil law country (Italy). My nomadic existence could I suppose be tendered as evidence in mitigation of any partiality I may be guilty of exhibiting in these pages.

Fortuitously, two of these jurisdictions are especially instructive; both underwent seismic transformations during the 1990s, entailing fundamental legal change. In 1992 the legal edifice of apartheid was demolished; two years later Nelson Mandela was elected President of the 'new' South Africa – with its democratic constitution, bill of rights, and constitutional court. And in 1997 Hong Kong was 'returned' to China; its metamorphosis from British colony to Chinese Special Administrative Region was, above all, a matter of law. The form and structure of this improbable creature – a capitalist enclave within a socialist state – is preserved by Hong Kong's new constitution, the Basic Law, which guarantees the continuation of the existing common law.

If there is a lesson to be learned from these two dramatic episodes, it is the perhaps rather prosaic truth that the law is an imperfect yet indispensable vehicle by which both to conserve and transform society. It would be rash to undervalue the certainty, generality, and predictability that an effective legal system can provide. Few societies achieve genuine harmony and accord; yet in the absence of law a descent into chaos and conflict would surely be an inevitable consequence for our increasingly polarized planet.

To abridge – without oversimplification – the central characteristics of the law entailed countless cold-blooded judgments. Numerous chunks were reluctantly dispatched to my swelling recycle bin. I can only hope that in charting the central terrain of contemporary law, the frontiers I have drawn are neither excessively narrow nor unreasonably wide. I have endeavoured to plot the most prominent features of the topography of the ever-shifting landscape of the law, acknowledging, of course, that much lies on its periphery.

It is important also to emphasize that law cannot properly be understood without an awareness of its social, political, moral, and economic dimensions. Legal theory or jurisprudence seeks to uncover many of these deeper philosophical elements that explain the complex phenomenon of law and its operation in legal systems. Chapter 3 attempts to illustrate the controversial tension between law and the moral practices adopted by society. I have resisted further excursions through the frequently impenetrable thicket of legal philosophy, both because it lies beyond the modest objectives of this work, and in the hope that readers in pursuit of an introduction to this stimulating discipline may wish to turn to my *Philosophy of Law: A Very Short Introduction* (Oxford University Press, 2006), which might be regarded as a companion volume to the one in your hands.

In hatching and executing this plot, those at Oxford University Press have, as before, been agreeable co-conspirators. Special thanks to Andrea Keegan, James Thompson, Alice Jacobs,

List of illustrations

Chapter 1
Law's roots

Step on a bus. The law is there. You have almost certainly entered into a contract to pay the fare to your destination. Alight before you have paid and the long arm of the criminal law may be expected to pursue you. The bus is involved in an accident. The law is ready to determine who is responsible for the injury you sustained. Your job, your home, your relationships, your very life – and your death, all – and more – are managed, controlled, and directed by the law. The legal system lies at the heart of any society, protecting rights, imposing duties, and establishing a framework for the conduct of almost every social, political, and economic activity. Punishing offenders, compensating the injured, and enforcing agreements are merely some of the tasks of a modern legal system. In addition, it endeavours to achieve justice, promote freedom, uphold the rule of law, and protect security.

To the layman, however, the law often seems a highly technical, bewildering mystery, with its antiquated and sometimes impenetrable jargon, obsolete procedures, and interminable stream of Byzantine statutes, subordinate legislation, and judgments of the courts. Lawyers tend to look backwards. The doctrine of precedent, hallmark of the common law, dictates that what has gone before is what now should be, thereby affording a measure of certainty and predictability in a precarious world.

But the law does not stand still. Globalization, rapid advances in technology, and the growth of administrative regulation place increasing strain on the law. Domestic legal systems are expected to respond to, and even anticipate, these changes, while many look to international law to settle disputes between states, punish malevolent dictators, and create a better world. These are among the numerous challenges to which contemporary legal systems are meant to rise.

The law is rarely uncontroversial. While lawyers and politicians habitually venerate its merits, reformers bewail its inadequacies, and sceptics refute the law's often self-righteous espousal of justice, liberty, and the rule of law. Few, however, would deny that, in most societies, law has become a significant instrument for progress and improvement in our social, political, moral, and economic life. Think of the transformation that legal rules have wrought in respect of numerous aspects of our lives that were once considered personal: the promotion of sexual and racial equality, safety at work and play, healthier food, candour in commerce, and a host of other admirable aspirations. Laws to protect human rights, the environment, and our personal security have mushroomed. Nothing seems beyond the reach of the long arm of the law. This boom in the law-making business renders it impractical both for citizens to become acquainted with its myriad rules, and for the authorities to enforce them.

The law is news. Murders, mergers, marriages, misfortunes, and mendacity are daily media fodder, especially when the misbehaviour is played out in court. Sensationalist trials concerning celebrities are, alas, only the small tip of a large iceberg. Lawsuits are a negligible part of the law, as will become evident in the following chapters.

But what is law? In very broad terms, two principal answers have been given to this deceptively simple question. On the one hand is the view that law consists of a set of universal moral principles in accordance with nature. This view (adopted by so-called natural lawyers) has a long history dating back to ancient Greece. For so-called legal positivists, on the other hand, law is nothing more than a collection of valid rules, commands, or norms that may lack any moral content. Others perceive the law as fundamentally a vehicle for the protection of individual rights, the attainment of justice, or economic, political, and sexual equality. Few believe that the law can be divorced from its social context. The social, political, moral, and economic dimensions of the law are essential to a proper understanding of its workaday operation. This is especially true in times of change. It is important to recognize the fragility of formalism; we skate on dangerously thin ice when we neglect the contingent nature of the law and its values. Reflection upon the nature of law may sometimes seem disconcertingly abstruse. More than occasionally, however, it reveals important insights into who we are and what we do. The nature and consequences of these different positions should become apparent before long.

The genesis of law

Despite the importance of law in society, its manifestation in the form of general codes first appears only around 3000 BC. Prior to the advent of writing, laws exist only in the form of custom. And the absence of written law retards the capacity of these rules to provide lasting or extensive application.

Among the first written codes is that of Hammurabi, king and creator of the Babylonian empire. It appeared in about 1760 BC, and is one of the earliest instances of a ruler proclaiming a systematic corpus of law to his people so that they are able to know their rights and duties. Engraved on a black stone slab (that may be seen in the Louvre in Paris), the code contains some 300 sections with rules relating to a broad array of activities ranging from the punishment that is to be inflicted on a false witness (death) to that to be meted out to a builder whose house collapses

3

1. The Code of Hammurabi, created by the King of Babylon in about 1760 BC, is among the earliest extant collection of laws. It is a well-preserved diorite stele setting out 282 laws, providing a fascinating insight into social life under his rule

killing the owner (death). The code is almost entirely devoid of defences or excuses, a very early example of strict liability!

The king was, in fact, acknowledging the existence of even earlier laws (of which we have only the barest of evidence), which his code implies. In truth, therefore, the code echoes customs that preceded the reign of this ancient monarch.

A more striking example of early law-making may be found in the laws of the Athenian statesman Solon in the 6th century BC. Regarded by the ancient Greeks as one of the Seven Wise Men, he was granted the authority to legislate to assist Athens in overcoming its social and economic crisis. His laws were extensive, including significant reforms to the economy, politics, marriage, and crime and punishment. He divided Athenian society into five classes based on financial standing. One's obligations (including tax liability) depended on one's class. He cancelled debts for which the peasants had pledged their land or their bodies, thereby terminating the institution of serfdom.

To resolve disputes between higher- and lower-ranked citizens, the Romans, in about 450 BC, issued, in tablet form, a compilation of laws known as the Twelve Tables. A commission of ten men (*Decemviri*) was appointed in about 455 BC to draft a code of law binding on all Romans (the privileged class – the patricians – and the common people – the plebeians) which the magistrates (two consuls) were required to enforce. The result was a compilation of numerous statutes, most derived from prevailing custom, that filled ten bronze tablets. The plebeians were unimpressed with the result, and a second commission of ten was appointed in 450 BC. It added another two tablets.

During the period of the so-called classical jurists, between the 1st century BC and the middle of the 3rd century AD, Roman law achieved a condition of considerable sophistication. Indeed, so prolific were these jurists (Gauis, Ulpian, Papinian, Paul, and

2. The Byzantine Roman Emperor Justinian, depicted here in one of the striking mosaics in the Basilica of San Vitale in Ravenna, oversaw the revision and codification of Roman law into the *Corpus Juris Civilis*, consisting of the Digest (or Pandects), the Institutes, the Codex, and the Novellae

several others) that their enormous output became hopelessly unwieldy. Between 529 and 534 AD, therefore, the Eastern emperor, Justinian, ordered that these manifold texts be reduced to a systematic, comprehensive codification. The three resulting books, the *Corpus Juris Civilis* (comprising the Digest, Codex, and Institutes), were to be treated as definitive: a conclusive statement of the law that required no interpretation. But this illusion of unconditional certainty soon became evident: the codification was both excessively lengthy (close to a million words) and too detailed to admit of easy application.

Its meticulous detail proved, however, to be its huge strength. More than 600 years after the fall of the Western Roman Empire, Europe witnessed a revival in the study of Roman law. And Justinian's codification, which had remained in force in parts of Western Europe, was the perfect specimen upon which European lawyers could conduct their experiments. With the establishment

3. The University of Bologna is arguably the first in the Western world. It was established around 1088, at which time masters of grammar, rhetoric, and logic began to turn their attention to the law. The University continues to boast a distinguished faculty of law

in about AD 1088 in Bologna of the first university in Western Europe, and the burgeoning of universities throughout Europe in the succeeding four centuries, students of law were taught Justinian's law alongside canon law. Moreover, the contradictions and complexity of the codes turned out to be an advantage, since the rules were, despite the emperor's fantasy of finality, susceptible to interpretation and adaptation in order to suit the requirements of the time. In this way, Roman civil law spread throughout most of Europe – in the face of its detractors during the Renaissance and the Reformation.

By the 18th century, however, it was recognized that more concise codes were called for. Justinian's codification was replaced by several codes that sought brevity, accessibility, and comprehensiveness. The Napoleonic code of 1804 came close to fulfilling these lofty aspirations. It was exported by colonization to large tracts of Western and Southern Europe and thence to Latin America, and it exerted an enormous influence throughout Europe. A more technical, abstract code was enacted in Germany in 1900. What it lacks in user-friendliness, it makes up for in its astonishing comprehensiveness. Known as the BGB, its influence

The appeal of codification

[A] man need but open the book in order to inform himself what the aspect borne by the law bears to every imaginable act that can come within the possible sphere of human agency: what acts it is his duty to perform for the sake of himself, his neighbour or the public: what acts he has a right to do, what other acts he has a right to have others perform for his advantage. … In this one repository the whole system of the obligations which either he or any one else is subject to are recorded and displayed to view.

Jeremy Bentham, *Of Laws in General*, chapter 19, para 10; quoted in Gerald J. Postema, *Bentham and the Common Law Tradition* (OUP, 1986), p. 148

has also been considerable: it afforded a model for the civil codes of China, Japan, Taiwan, Greece, and the Baltic states.

The Western legal tradition

The Western legal tradition has a number of distinctive features, in particular:

- A fairly clear demarcation between legal institutions (including adjudication, legislation, and the rules they spawn), on the one hand, and other types of institutions, on the other; legal authority in the former exerting supremacy over political institutions.

- The nature of legal doctrine which comprises the principal source of the law and the basis of legal training, knowledge, and institutional practice.

- The concept of law as a coherent, organic body of rules and principles with its own internal logic.

- The existence and specialized training of lawyers and other legal personnel.

While some of these characteristics may occur in other legal traditions, they differ in respect of both the importance they accord to, and their attitude towards, the precise role of law in society. Law, especially the rule of law, in Western Europe is a fundamental element in the formation and significance of society itself. This veneration of law and the legal process shapes also the exercise of government, domestically and internationally, by contemporary Western democracies.

The ideal of the rule of law is most closely associated with the English constitutional scholar Albert Venn Dicey, who in his celebrated work *An Introduction to the Study of the Law of the Constitution*, published in 1885, expounded the fundamental precepts of the (unwritten) British constitution, and especially the concept of the rule of law which, in his view, consisted of the following three principles:

- The absolute supremacy or predominance of regular law as opposed to the influence of arbitrary power.

- Equality before the law or the equal subjection of all classes to the ordinary law of the land administered by the ordinary courts.

- The law of the constitution is a consequence of the rights of individuals as defined and enforced by the courts.

The antique charm of the common law

[W]hat the Continental lawyer sees as being a single problem and solves with a single institution is seen by the common lawyer as being a bundle of more specific problems which he solves with a plurality of legal institutions, most of them of ancient pedigree ... One should be frank enough to say, however, that though the English system has a certain antiquarian charm about it, it is so extremely complex and difficult to understand that no one else would dream of adopting it.

K. Zweigert and H. Kötz,
An Introduction to Comparative Law, 3rd edn (OUP, 1998), p. 37

Civil law and common law

The system of codified law that obtains in most of Europe, South America, and elsewhere (see Figure 4) is known as civil law, in contrast to the common law system that applies in England, former British colonies, the United States, and most of Canada. Civil law is frequently divided into four groups. First, is French civil law, which obtains also in Belgium and Luxembourg, the Canadian province of Quebec, Italy, Spain, and their former colonies, including those in Africa and South America. Second, German civil law, which is, in large part, applied in Austria, Switzerland, Portugal, Greece, Turkey, Japan, South Korea, and Taiwan. Third, Scandinavian civil law exists in Sweden, Denmark, Norway, and Iceland. Finally, Chinese (or China) law combines elements of civil law and socialist law. This is by no means an airtight classification. For example, Italian, Portuguese, and Brazilian law have, over the last century, moved closer to German law as their civil codes increasingly adopted key elements of the German civil code. The Russian civil code is partly a translation of the Dutch code.

Though the two traditions – common law and civil law – have, over the last century, grown closer, there are at least five significant differences between the two systems. First, the common law is essentially unwritten, non-textual law that was fashioned by medieval lawyers and the judges of the royal courts before whom they submitted their arguments. Indeed, it may be that this entrenched oral tradition, supported by a strong monarchy, developed by experts before the revival in the study of Roman law, explains why that system was never 'received' in England.

Codification has been resisted by generations of common lawyers, though this hostility has been weaker in the United States, where since its establishment in 1923, the American Law Institute (a group of lawyers, judges, and legal scholars) has published a number of 'restatements of the law' (including those on contract, property, agency, torts, and trusts) to 'address uncertainty in the law through a restatement of basic legal subjects that would tell judges and lawyers what the law was'. They seek to clarify rather than codify the law. Their standing as secondary authority is demonstrated by their widespread (though not always consistent) acceptance by American courts. More significant is the Uniform Commercial Code (UCC) which establishes consistent rules in respect of a number of key commercial transactions that apply

11

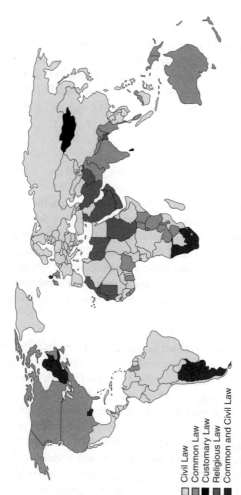

4. While civil law is the world's most ubiquitous system, the common law and, to a lesser extent, religious and customary law, are applied in a number of countries

Civil Law
Common Law
Customary Law
Religious Law
Common and Civil Law

across the country. With 50 states with different laws, uniformity in respect of commercial transactions is obviously vital. Imagine the confusion in the absence of such standardization: you live in New York and buy a car in New Jersey that is made in Michigan, warehoused in Maine, and delivered to your home.

Second, the common law is casuistic: the building blocks are cases rather than, as in the civil law system, texts. Ask any American, Australian, or Antiguan law student how most of his or her study-time is spent. The answer will almost certainly be 'reading cases'. Question their counterparts from Argentina, Austria, or Algeria, and they will allude to the civil and penal codes they persistently peruse. The consequence of the common lawyer's preoccupation with what the judges say – rather than what the codes declare – is a more pragmatic, less theoretical approach to legal problem-solving.

Third, in view of the centrality of court decisions, the common law elevates the doctrine of precedent to a supreme position in the legal system. This doctrine means both that previous decisions of courts that involve substantially similar facts ought to govern present cases and that the judgments of higher courts are binding on those lower in the judicial hierarchy. The justification for the idea is that it engenders constancy, predictability, and objectivity, while allowing for judges to 'distinguish' apparently binding precedents on the ground that the case before them differs from them in some material respect.

A fourth generalization is that while the common law proceeds from the premise 'where there is a remedy, there is a right', the civil law tradition generally adopts the opposite position: 'where there is a right, there is a remedy'. If the common law is essentially remedial, rather than rights-based, in its outlook, this is plainly a result of the so-called writ system under which, from the 12th century in England, litigation could not commence without a writ issued on the authority of the king. Every claim had its own formal writ. So, for example, the writ of debt was a prerequisite to any action to recover money owing, and the writ of right existed to recover land. In the 17th century, the writ of *habeas corpus* (literally 'you must produce the body') was a vital check on arbitrary power, for it required the production of a person detained without trial to be brought before a court. In the absence of a legal justification for his imprisonment, the judge could order the individual to be liberated. It took a century for civil law jurisdictions to accept this fundamental attribute of a free society.

Finally, in the 13th century, the common law introduced trial by jury for both criminal and civil cases. The jury decides on the facts of the case; the judge determines the law. Trial by jury has remained a fundamental feature of the common law. This separation between facts and law was never adopted by civil law systems. It illustrates also the importance of the oral tradition of common law as against the essential role of written argument employed by the civil law.

The common law, chaos, and codification

[L]ife might be much simpler if the common law consisted of a code of rules, identifiable by reference to source rules, but the reality of the matter is that it is all much more chaotic than that, and the only way to make the common law conform to the ideal would be to codify the system, which would then cease to be common law at all. The myth, for that is what it is, owes its attractiveness to another ideal, that of the rule of law, not men. ... It consequently distorts the nature of the system to conceive of the common law as a set of rules, an essentially precise notion, as if one could in principle both state the rules of the common law and count them like so many sheep, or engrave them on tablets of stone.

A. W. B. Simpson, 'The Common Law and Legal Theory', in William Twining (ed.), *Legal Theory and Common Law* (Blackwell, 1986), pp. 15–16

There are also certain jurisdictions, such as Scotland, that, though their legal systems are not codified, preserve varying degrees of Roman influence. On the other hand, some jurisdictions have avoided the impact of Roman law, but because of the prominence of legislation, these systems resemble the civil law tradition. They include Scandinavian countries, which inhabit an unusual place in the 'Romano-Germanic' family.

Other legal traditions

Religious law

No legal system can be properly understood without investigating its religious roots. These roots are often both deep and durable. Indeed, the Roman Catholic Church has the longest, continuously operating legal system in the Western world. The influence of religion is palpable in the case of Western legal systems:

> [B]asic institutions, concepts, and values... have their sources in religious rituals, liturgies, and doctrines of the eleventh and twelfth centuries, reflecting new attitudes toward death, sin, punishment, forgiveness, and salvation, as well as new assumptions concerning the relationship of the divine to the human and of faith to reason.

In Europe in the 12th century, ecclesiastical law played an important role in a number of fields. Ecclesiastical courts claimed jurisdiction over a wide range of matters, including heresy, fornication, homosexuality, adultery, defamation, and perjury. Canon law still governs several churches, especially the Roman Catholic Church, the Eastern Orthodox Church, and the Anglican Communion of Churches.

The rise of secularism has not completely extinguished the impact of religious law. The jurisdiction of Western legislatures and courts over exclusively religious matters is frequently curtailed, and many legal systems incorporate religious law or delegate to

> ## Talmudic law
>
> [The Talmud] represents a brilliant intellectual concept, a
> book of law which contains endless differences of opinion
> from all ages and dealing with all that had gone on before,
> while seen as never definitely finished and thus leaving room
> for still more opinion, as each age engages with it. There is no
> equivalent to it in any legal tradition.
>
> H. Patrick Glenn, *On Common Laws* (OUP, 2005), p. 131

religious institutions matters of a domestic nature. Nevertheless,
one of the hallmarks of Western legality is the separation between
church and state.

While a number of prominent religious legal traditions co-exist
with state systems of law, some have actually been adopted as
state law. The most significant are Talmudic, Islamic, and Hindu
law. All three derive their authority from a divine source: the
exposition of religious doctrine as revealed in the Talmud, Koran,
and Vedas respectively.

> ## Hindu law
>
> Hindu law recognizes the possibility of change, both of law
> and the world, but ... [i]t just tolerates it, without in any way
> encouraging it, as something that's going to happen, but
> which shouldn't disturb the basic harmony of the world. If
> it does, it's bad karma, and this too will be dealt with. Thus,
> for a written tradition, Hindu tradition is incredibly roomy.
> Toleration is not at the perimeter of it, but at the centre. And
> toleration turns out to have its own kind of discipline.
>
> H. Patrick Glenn, *Legal Traditions of the World*, 2nd edn (OUP, 2004), p. 287

All have influenced secular law in a variety of ways. For example, Talmudic law had a significant impact on Western commercial, civil, and criminal law. In addition to common and civil law systems, it is possible to identify four other significant legal traditions.

Islamic law (or the *Sharia*) is based largely on the teachings of the Koran. It extends to all aspects of life, not merely those that pertain to the state or society. It is observed by more than one-fifth of the population of the world, some 1.3 billion people.

At its core, Hinduism postulates the notion of *Kharma*: goodness and evil on earth determine the nature of one's next existence. Hindu law, especially in relation to family law and succession, applies to around 900 million individuals, mostly in living in India.

Islamic law

Islamic law ... seeks constancy with common-sense assumptions about humanity, not through the refinement of categories of its own creation. [It] is a system of adjudication, of ethics and of logic that finds its touchstone not in the perfecting of doctrine, but in the standards of everyday life, and measured in this way it is enormously developed, integrated, logical and successful. Man's duty is to conform to God's moral limits, not to try to invent them. But within these limits established by God one can create relationships and traffic in the knowledge of their existence, intricacies and repercussions.

Lawrence Rosen, *The Anthropology of Justice: Law as Culture in Islamic Society* (CUP, 1989), p. 56; quoted in Malise Ruthven, *Islam: A Very Short Introduction* (OUP, 1997), p. 89

Customary law

To constitute custom, the practices involved require something beyond mere usage or habit. They need to have a degree of legality. This is not always easy to discern, though customary law continues to play an important role, especially in jurisdictions with mixed legal systems such as occur in several African countries. The tenacity of custom is evident also in India and China. Indeed, in respect of the latter, the Basic Law of the Special Administrative Region of Hong Kong provides that customary law, as part of the laws previously in force in Hong Kong (prior to 1 July 1997), shall be maintained.

Mixed legal systems

In some jurisdictions two or more systems interact. In South Africa, for example, the existence of Roman-Dutch law is a consequence of the influence of Dutch jurists who drew on Roman law in their writing. This tradition was exported to the Cape Colony in the 17th and 18th centuries. The hybrid nature of South Africa's legal system is especially vivid, since, following the arrival of English common law in the 19th century, the two systems co-existed in a remarkable exercise of legal harmony. And they continue to do so:

> Like a jewel in a brooch, the Roman-Dutch law in South Africa today glitters in a setting that was made in England. Even if it were true (which it is not) that the whole of South African private law and criminal law had remained pure Roman-Dutch law, the South African legal system as a whole would still be a hybrid one, in which civil- and common-law elements jostle with each other.

The mixture is no longer nearly as effective in Sri Lanka or Guyana, to where Roman-Dutch law was exported in 1799 and 1803 respectively, but where the common law now predominates.

Chinese law

Traditional Chinese society, in common with other Confucian civilizations, did not develop a system of law founded by the ideas that underlie Western legal systems. Confucianism adopted the concept of '*li*': an intense opposition to any system of fixed rules that applied universally and equally. Though Chinese 'legalists' sought to undermine the political authority of this Confucian philosophy of persuasion by championing 'rule by law' ('*fa*') in place of the organic order of the Confucian '*li*', the latter continues to dominate China.

The spectacular modernization of China has generated a need for laws that facilitate its economic and financial development. But this new legalism has not been accompanied by an ideological partiality for law along Western lines. The role of law in modern

The future of the law in China

I would venture to suggest that as economic and social changes sweep through China as a result of the current economic reforms, the social context for the closed elements of traditional legal culture will, in the course of time, be replaced by a context more favourable to elements more consistent with liberalism, democracy, human rights, and the rule of law. They will thus find their place in a rejuvenated Chinese culture, which can and will continue to be informed and inspired by the open elements of the Chinese tradition, such as Confucian benevolence, moral self-cultivation, and the quiet but unending spiritual quest for harmony of 'heaven, earth, humanity and the myriad things'.

Albert H. Y. Chen, 'Confucian Legal Culture and its Modern Fate', in Raymond Wacks (ed.), *The New Legal Order in Hong Kong* (Hong Kong University Press, 1999), pp. 532–3

China remains decidedly instrumental and pragmatic. Its system is essentially civilian and hence largely codified, but this has not yet engendered either greater esteem for the law or a diminution in the control of the Communist Party.

The allure of the law

Individuals aggrieved by iniquity often complain, 'There ought to be a law against that!' There is an understandable tendency to look to the law to resolve our problems. And the law's failure to provide a remedy may provoke a sense of frustration and anger. Yet legal regulation of antisocial behaviour is not as simple as it may appear, as should become clear when the challenges to the law of technology are considered in Chapter 6. Before we reach for the law – or a lawyer – it is worth recalling the words of the great American judge Learned Hand, who prescribed this antidote to an excessive faith in the law:

> I often wonder whether we do not rest our hopes too much upon constitutions, upon laws and upon courts. These are false hopes; believe me, these are false hopes. Liberty lies in the hearts of men and women; when it dies there, no constitution, no law, no court can even do much to help it. While it lies there it needs no constitution, no law, no court to save it.

The validity or otherwise of this assertion should become evident in the course of these pages.

The functions of law

Order

Football, chess, bridge are unthinkable without rules. A casual poker club could not function without an agreed set of rules by which its members are expected abide. It is not surprising therefore that when they are formed into larger social groups, humans have always required laws. Without law, society is barely conceivable. We tend, unfortunately, towards egoism. The restraint that law imposes on our liberty is the price we pay for living in a community. 'We are slaves of the law' wrote the great Roman lawyer Cicero, 'so that we may be free'. And the law has provided the security and self-determination that has, in large part, facilitated social and political advancement.

The cliché 'law and order' is perhaps more accurately rendered 'law *for* order'. Without law, it is widely assumed, order would be unattainable. And order – or what is now popularly called 'security' – is the central aim of most governments. It is an essential prerequisite of a society that aspires to safeguard the well-being of its members.

Thomas Hobbes famously declared that in his natural state – prior to the social contract – the condition of man was 'solitary, poor, nasty, brutish and short', though more than one student has rendered this maxim as '… nasty, *British* and short'. Law and government are required, Hobbes argues, if we are to preserve order and security. We therefore need, by the social contract, to surrender our natural freedom in order to create an orderly society. His philosophy is nowadays regarded as somewhat authoritarian, placing order above justice. In particular, his theory – indeed, his self-confessed purpose – is to undermine the legitimacy of revolutions against even malevolent governments.

He recognizes that we are fundamentally equal, mentally and physically: even the weakest has the strength to kill the strongest. This equality, he suggests, engenders discord. We tend to quarrel, he argues, for three main reasons: competition (for limited supplies of material possessions), distrust, and glory (we remain hostile in order to preserve our powerful reputations). As a consequence of our inclination towards conflict, Hobbes concludes that we are in a natural state of continuous war of all against all, where no morals exist, and all live in perpetual fear. Until this state of war ceases, all have a right to everything, including another person's life. Order is, of course, only one part of the functions of law story.

Justice

Though the law unquestionably protects order, it has another vital purpose. In the words of the 20th-century English judge Lord Denning:

> The law as I see it has two great objects: to preserve order and to do justice; and the two do not always coincide. Those whose training lies towards order, put certainty before justice; whereas those whose training lies toward the redress of grievances, put justice before certainty. The right solution lies in keeping the proper balance between the two.

The pursuit of justice must lie at the heart of any legal system. The virtual equation of law with justice has a long history. It is to be found in the writing of the Greek philosophers, in the Bible, and in the Roman Emperor Justinian's codification of the law. The quest for clarity in the analysis of the concept of justice has, however, not been unproblematic. Both Plato and Aristotle sought to illuminate its principal features. Indeed, Aristotle's approach remains the launching pad for most discussions of justice. He argues that justice consists in treating equals equally and 'unequals' unequally, in proportion to their inequality. Acknowledging that the equality implied in justice could be either arithmetical (based on the identity of the persons concerned) or geometrical (based on maintaining the same proportion), Aristotle distinguishes between corrective or commutative justice, on the one hand, and distributive justice, on the other. The former is the justice of the courts which is applied in the redress of crimes or civil wrongs. It requires that all men are to be treated equally. The latter (distributive justice), he argues, concerns giving each according to his desert or merit. This, in Aristotle's view, is principally the concern of the legislator.

In his celebrated book, *The Concept of Law*, H. L. A. Hart maintains that the idea of justice:

> ... consists of two parts: a uniform or constant feature, summarised in the precept 'Treat like cases alike' and a shifting or varying criterion used in determining when, for any given purpose, cases are alike or different.

He contends that in the modern world the principle that human beings are entitled to be treated alike has become so well established that racial discrimination is usually defended on the ground that those discriminated against are not 'fully human'.

An especially influential theory of justice is utilitarianism, which is always associated with the famous English philosopher and law reformer Jeremy Bentham. In his characteristically animated language:

> Nature has placed mankind under the governance of two sovereign masters, *pain* and *pleasure*. It is for them alone to point out what we ought to do, as well as to determine what we shall do. On the one hand the standard of right and wrong, on the other the chain of causes and effects, are fastened to their throne. ... The *principle of utility* recognizes this subjection, and assumes it for the foundation of that system, the object of which is to rear the fabric of felicity by the hands of reason and of law. Systems which attempt to question it, deal in sounds instead of sense, in caprice instead of reason, in darkness instead of light.

To this end, Bentham formulated a 'felicific calculus' by which to assess the 'happiness factor' of any action.

There are numerous competing approaches to the meaning of justice, including those that echo Hobbes' social contract. A modern version is to be found in the important writings of John Rawls who, in rejecting utilitarianism, advances the idea of justice as fairness which seeks to arrive at objective principles of justice that would hypothetically be agreed upon by individuals who, under a veil of ignorance, do not know to which sex, class, religion, or social position they belong. Each person represents a social class, but they have no idea whether they are clever or dim, strong or weak. Nor do they know in which country or in what period they are living. They possess only certain elementary knowledge about the laws of science and psychology. In this state of blissful ignorance, they must unanimously decide upon a contract the general principles of which will define the terms under which they will live as a society. And, in doing so, they are moved by rational self-interest: each individual seeks those principles which will give him or her the best chance of attaining his chosen conception of the good life, whatever that happens to be.

Law

Realism about law

The life of the law has not been logic; it has been experience. The felt necessities of the time, the prevalent moral and political theories, intuitions of public policy, avowed or unconscious, even the prejudices which judges share with their fellow-men, have a good deal more to do than the syllogism in determining the rules by which men should be governed. The law embodies the story of a nation's development through many centuries, and it cannot be dealt with as if it contained only the axioms and corollaries of a book of mathematics.

Justice Oliver Wendell Holmes, *The Common Law*, 1

Justice is unlikely to be attained by a legal system unless its rules are, as far as possible, reasonable, general, equal, predictable, and certain. None of these objectives can be achieved in absolute terms; they are ideals. So, for example, the law can never be utterly certain. Occasionally the facts of a case are obscure and difficult to discover. Similarly, the law itself may not be easy to establish – especially for the non-lawyer faced with a profusion of statutes, decisions of the courts, by-laws, and so on. The Internet has rendered the task of finding the law slightly easier, but, in the face of an escalating spate of legal sources, it remains a formidable challenge. The maxim 'hard cases make bad law' expresses the important principle that is better that the law be certain than that it be bent to accommodate an unusual case.

Justice requires more than just laws; the process whereby justice is attained must be a fair one. This entails, first, an impartial, independent judicial system (discussed in Chapter 5). Second, there must be a competent and independent legal profession (also discussed in Chapter 5). Third, procedural justice is a vital ingredient of a just legal system. This necessitates, amongst other things, access to legal advice, assistance, and representation, and the guarantee of a fair trial (discussed in Chapter 4).

In a just or nearly just society, few obstacles beset the path of the judge who, in a general sense, seeks to advance the cause of justice. Heroism is rarely required. Where injustice pervades the legal system, however, the role of judge assumes a considerably more intractable form. How could a decent, moral, fair-minded person in a society such as Nazi Germany or apartheid South Africa square his conscience with his calling? This moral quandary is perhaps encountered also by ordinary individuals who inhabit an unjust society. Should the fact that the judge is a public official distinguish him from others who participate in the legal system or who simply derive benefit from its injustice? Are there compelling reasons for morally differentiating judges from others, particularly lawyers? The honourable judge attempts to do justice when he can, admitting that his autonomy is curtailed in several major areas of the law. But is a conscientious lawyer not in the same boat? He strives to do good, often at great personal cost, within the strictures of the legal system. He too lends legitimacy to the system. Is the moral dilemma not the same?

There are no simple answers to this sort of predicament. Institutionally, judges differ from lawyers: they are officers appointed or elected to implement the law. Their legal duty is plain. Lawyers, on the other hand, are not state officials. They owe a strong duty to their clients. They must, of course, work within the system, but their responsibility is to utilize the law, not to dispense justice. They may find the law morally repugnant, but their role within an unjust legal system is easier to justify than that of the judge. So, for example, lawyers in apartheid South Africa themselves recognized this distinction, and several prominent senior lawyers declared that on grounds of conscience they would decline appointment to the bench. Yet they continued as lawyers. And, though the temptation to withdraw from the system was often powerful, many lawyers played a courageous, sometimes heroic, part in the struggle for justice.

A lawyer may, however, decide that his or her participation in the legal system serves to legitimate it. This is a perfectly proper moral response. But it does not follow that the dilemma is therefore the same as for the state official. This is because of the important functional differences between the two. In particular, lawyers, unlike judges, are not concerned exclusively with the forensic process. Indeed, lawyers do some of their most worthwhile work when they advise clients of their rights, whether or not litigation is intended or anticipated (see Chapter 5). Thus, while appearance before the court may be regarded as a more palpable acceptance of its legitimacy, advising clients may not.

The law lays down certain ground rules. Murder is wrong. So is theft. Legal rules against these and other forms of antisocial behaviour are the most obvious, and the most conspicuous, instances of legal regulation. Modern governments seek to persuade us to behave well by means other than compulsion. Often the carrot replaces the stick. Advertising campaigns, official websites, and other forms of public relations exercises exhort us to do X or avoid Y. But by setting standards of conduct,

the law remains the most powerful tool in the hands of
the state.

Further, the law establishes a framework within which
unavoidable disputes may be resolved. Courts are the principal
forum for the resolution of conflict. Almost every legal system
includes courts or court-like bodies with the power to adjudicate
impartially upon a dispute and, following a recognized procedure,
to issue an authoritative judgment based on the law.

The law facilitates, often even encourages, certain social and
economic arrangements. It provides the rules to enable parties to
enter into the contract of marriage or employment or purchase
and sale. Company law, inheritance law, property law all furnish
the means by which we are able to pursue the countless activities
that constitute social life.

Another major function of the law is the protection of property.
Rules identify who owns what, and this, in turn, determines who
has the strongest right or claim to things. Not only does the law
thereby secure the independence of individuals, it also encourages
them to be more productive and creative (generating new ideas
that may be transformed into intellectual property, protected by
patents and copyright).

The law seeks also to protect the general well-being of the
community. Instead of individuals being compelled to fend for
themselves, the law oversees or coordinates public services that
would be beyond the capacity of citizens or the private sector to
achieve, such as defence or national security.

Another dimension of the law that has assumed enormous
proportions in recent years is the protection of individual rights.
For example, the law of many countries includes a bill of rights as
a means of seeking to protect individuals against the violation of
an inventory of rights that are considered fundamental. In some

cases a bill of rights is constitutionally entrenched. Entrenchment is a device which protects the bill of rights, placing it beyond the reach of simple legislative amendment. In other jurisdictions, rights are less secure when they are safeguarded by ordinary statutes that may be repealed like any other law. Almost every Western country (with the conspicuous exception of Australia) boasts a constitutional or legislative bill of rights.

The sources of law

Unlike manna, the law does not fall from the sky. It springs from recognized 'sources'. This reflects the idea that in the absence of some authoritative source, a rule that purports to be a law will not be accepted as a law. Lawyers therefore speak of 'authority'. 'What', a judge may ask a lawyer, 'is your authority for that proposition?' In reply, the common lawyer is likely to cite either a previous decision of a court or a statute. A civil lawyer will refer the court to an article of, say, the civil code. In either case, the existence of an acknowledged source will be decisive in the formulation of a legal argument.

In addition to these two conventional sources of law, it is not uncommon for the writings of legal academics to be recognized as authoritative sources of law. There are also certain sources that are, strictly speaking, non-legal, including (though it may be hard to believe) common sense and moral values.

Legislation

The stereotypical source of law in contemporary legal systems is the statute enacted by a legislative body that seeks to introduce new rules, or to amend old ones – generally in the name of reform, progress, or the alleged improvement of our lives. Legislation is, however, of quite recent origin. The 20th century witnessed an eruption of legislative energy by law-makers who frequently owe their election to a manifesto of promises that presumes the existence of an unrelenting statutory assembly line. In most advanced societies, it is not easy to think of any sphere of life untouched by the dedication of legislators to manage what we may or may not do.

Statutes are rarely a panacea; indeed, they not infrequently achieve the precise opposite of what their draftsmen intended. Moreover, language is seldom adequately lucid or precise not to require interpretation. The words of a statute are rarely conclusive; they are susceptible of different construction – especially where lawyers are concerned. Inevitably, therefore, it falls to judges to construe the meaning of statutes. And when they do so, they normally create precedents that provide guidance for courts that may be faced with the interpretation of the legislation in the future.

A number of technical 'rules' have developed to assist judges to decode the intention of law-makers. A classic example that demonstrates the various approaches to the legislative interpretation is a hypothetical statute that prohibits 'vehicles' from entering the park. This plainly includes a motor car, but what about a bicycle? Or a skateboard? One solution is to adopt the so-called 'literal' or 'textual' approach which accords the text in question its ordinary everyday meaning. Thus the definition of a 'vehicle' would not extend beyond an automobile, a truck, or a bus; bicycles and skateboards are not, in any ordinary sense, vehicles. Where, however, the plain meaning gives rise to an absurd result, its proponents concede that the approach runs into trouble, and the words or phrases in issue will need to be interpreted in a manner that avoids obvious illogicality.

A second approach seeks to discover the *purpose* of the legislation. In our example, we may conclude that the purpose of the provision is to secure the peace and quiet of the park. If so, we are likely to find it easier to decide what is the real intention of the legislation, and hence to distinguish between a car (noisy) and a bicycle (quiet). This approach also permits judges to consider the wider purposes of the legal system. Where either the narrow or broader purpose suggests an interpretation different from the literal meaning of the language, the purposive approach would prefer a liberal to a literal interpretation.

It is an approach that holds sway in several jurisdictions. Courts in the United States routinely scrutinize the legislative history of statutes in order to resolve ambiguity or confirm their plain meaning. A similar approach is evident in Canada and Australia. And under the European Communities Act of 1972, a court is required to adopt a purposive approach in construing legislation that implements European Community (EC) law. Indeed, since EC legislation tends to be drafted along civil law lines – expressed in fewer words than common law statutes, but with a high degree of abstraction – a purposive approach is unavoidable, and broad social and economic objectives are frequently considered by the courts. The European Court of Justice also tends to favour a purposive approach.

It is, I think, fair to say, that there is no single ideal approach to unlock the door to an ideal construction of a statute. Indeed, there is considerable doubt as to whether the 'rules' are, or can be, uniformly applied. No less a distinguished author on statutory interpretation than Professor Sir Rupert Cross shared the doubts expressed by his Oxford pupils:

> Each and every pupil told me there were three rules – the literal rule, the golden rule and the mischief rule, and that the courts invoke whichever of them is believed to do justice in the particular case. I had, and still have, my doubts, but what was most disconcerting was the fact that whatever question I put to pupils or examinees elicited the same reply. Even if the question was What is meant by 'the intention of Parliament?' or What are the principal extrinsic aids to interpretation? Back came the answer as of yore: 'There are three rules of interpretation – the literal rule…'

Common law rules of statutory interpretation

The literal rule

If the language of a statute be plain, admitting of only one meaning, the Legislature must be taken to have meant and intended what it has plainly expressed, and whatever it has in clear terms enacted must be enforced though it should lead to absurd or mischievous results.

Lord Atkinson in *Vacher v London Society of Compositors* [1913] A.C. 107, 1211

The golden (or purposive) rule

[The] golden rule ... is that we are to take the whole statute together, and construe it all together, giving the words their ordinary signification, unless when so applied they produce an inconsistency, or an absurdity or inconvenience so great as to convince the Court that the intention could not have been to use them in their ordinary signification, and to justify the Court in putting on them some other signification, which though less proper, is one which the Court thinks the words will bear.

Lord Blackburn in *River Wear Commissioners v Adamson* (1877) 2 App Cas 743, 764–5

The mischief rule (or the rule in Heydon's Case)

In applying the mischief rule, the court is required to ask four questions: (1) What was the common law before the statute was passed? (2) What was the defect or mischief for which the common law did not provide? (3) What remedy did the legislature intend to provide? (4) What was the true reason for that remedy?

Heydon's Case (1584) 3 Co Rep 7a, 7b

Moreover, there are those who cynically contend that the rules simply justify solutions reached on wholly different grounds.

Another difficulty intrinsic to the legislative process is that law-makers cannot be expected to predict the future. Legislation designed to achieve a specific objective may fail when a new situation arises. This is especially true when innovative technology materializes to confound the law. Some of the awkward challenges to the legislation on copyright or pornography posed by the rise of digital technology and the Internet are discussed in Chapter 6.

Common law

One normally associates the phrase 'common law' with *English* common law. But common laws, in the sense of laws other than those particular to a specific jurisdiction, largely in the form of legislation, are not peculiar to England and English-speaking former colonies. Numerous forms of common law have existed, and endure, in several European legal systems, including France, Italy, Germany, and Spain. They developed from Roman roots and achieved their commonality by indigenous reception instead of imposition. In England, however, the judge-driven common law tended to be defined in jurisdictional and remedial terms. But though the common laws of Europe (Germany, France) seem to have transmogrified into national laws, they are not dead. Despite the advent of codification and the doctrine of precedent these – non-English – common laws, though battered and bruised, still survive. And they circulate tirelessly through the veins of various legal systems.

In respect of the common law of England – and those many countries to which it has been exported – previous decisions of courts (judicial precedents) are a fundamental source of law. The doctrine of precedent stipulates that the reasoning deployed by courts in earlier cases is normally binding on courts who subsequently hear similar cases. The idea is based on the principle '*stare decisis*' ('let the decision stand'). It is, of course, designed to promote the stability and predictability of the law, as well as ensuring that like cases are, as far as possible, treated alike.

Every common law jurisdiction has its distinctive hierarchy of courts, and the doctrine of precedent requires courts to follow the decisions of courts higher up the totem pole. In doing so, however, the lower court need follow only the *reasoning* employed by the higher tribunal in reaching its decision – the so-called *ratio decidendi*. Any other statements made by the judges are not binding: they are 'things said by the way' (*obiter dicta*). For example, a judge may give his opinion on the case, which is not relevant to the material facts. Or she may pontificate on the social context in which the case arose. In neither case need a subsequent judge regard these utterances as anything more than persuasive.

Discerning the *ratio decidendi* of a case is not infrequently an arduous journey through an impenetrable thicket. Judgments may be long and convoluted. Where the court consists of several judges, each may adduce different reasons to arrive at the same conclusion. Though judges and academics have supplied various road maps, there is no easy route. No simple formula is available to uncover the binding chunk of the judgment. As with much in life, it requires practice and experience.

The notion that previous decisions (often ancient) should determine the outcome of contemporary cases is occasionally ridiculed. Most famously, Jeremy Bentham stigmatized the doctrine of precedent as 'dog law':

> Whenever your dog does anything you want to break him of, you wait till he does it, and then beat him for it. This is the way you make laws for your dog: and this is the way the judges make law for you and me.... [T]he more antique the precedent – that is to say, the more barbarous, inexperienced, and prejudice-led the race of men,

by and among whom the precedent was set – the more unlike that the same *past* state of things ... is the *present* state of things.

It is frequently assumed that continental systems of law do not employ an equivalent doctrine of precedent under which judges are bound to follow decisions of a higher court. This is mistaken. In practice, a judgment of the French *Cour de Cassation* or the German *Bundesgerichtshof* will be followed by lower courts no less than the judgment of a common law court of appeal.

Other sources

In a perfect world the law would be clear, certain, and comprehensible. The reality is some way from this Utopian vision. Law in all jurisdictions is a dynamic organism subject to the vicissitudes of social, political, and moral values. One influential foundation of moral ideas has already been mentioned: natural law, the ancient philosophy that continues to shape the teachings of the Roman Catholic Church. As we saw, it proceeds from the assumption that there are principles that exist in the natural world that we, as rational beings, are capable of discovering by the exercise of reason. For instance, abortion is regarded as immoral on the ground that it offends natural law's respect for life.

In spite of the caricature of law, lawyers, and courts existing in an artificial, hermetically sealed bubble, judges do reach out into the real world and take account of public opinion. Indeed, on occasion courts respond with unseemly alacrity, such as when the media laments the alleged leniency of judges in a certain case or in respect of a particularly egregious offence. Judges may react rashly (dare one say injudiciously?) by flexing their sentencing muscles apparently to placate perceived public opinion.

More prudently, perhaps, courts, much to the gratification of academic lawyers, increasingly cite their scholarly colleagues' views as expressed in textbooks and learned journals. To be quoted in a judgment is recognition, not only that one's works are actually read, but also that they carry some weight.

In the absence of direct authority on a point of law, courts may even permit lawyers to refer to 'common sense' to support an argument. This might include widely accepted notions of right and wrong, generalizations about social practices, fairness, perceptions of the law, and other common conceptions that cynics occasionally represent as foreign to the legal process.

Chapter 2
Law's branches

The abundant branches of the law perpetually proliferate. As social life is transformed, the law is rarely far behind – to invent and define new concepts and rules, and to resolve the disputes that inevitably arise. Thus our brave new legal world continues to usher in novel subjects: space law, sports law, sex law. At the core of most legal systems, however, are the fundamental disciplines that hark back to the roots of law: the law of contract, tort, criminal law, and the law of property. To that nucleus must be added a horde of disciplines, including constitutional and administrative law, family law, public and private international law, environmental law, company law, commercial law, the law of evidence, succession, insurance law, labour law, intellectual property law, tax law, securities law, banking law, maritime law, welfare law, human rights law. To facilitate criminal and civil trials and other practical matters (such as the conveyance of land, the drafting of wills), complex rules of procedure have developed, spawning their own subcategories.

Public and private law

The distinction between public and private law is fundamental, especially to the civil law systems of Continental Europe and its former colonies. Though there is no general agreement as to precisely how or where the line should be drawn, it is fair to say that public law governs the relationship between citizen and state, while private law concerns that between individuals or groups in society. Thus, constitutional and administrative law is the archetypal example of public law, while the law of contract is one of many limbs of private law. Criminal law, since it largely involves prosecutions by the state against offenders, belongs also under the umbrella of public law. (All three branches are described below.) As the state intrudes more and more into our lives, however, the boundary between public and private law grows ever fuzzier.

Contract

Agreements are an indispensable element of social life. When you agree to meet me for a drink, borrow a book, or give me a lift to work, we have entered into an agreement. But the law will not compel you to turn up at the bar, return my book, or pick me up in your car. These social arrangements, while their breach may cause considerable inconvenience, distress, and even expense, fall short of a contract as understood by most legal systems.

One of the hallmarks of a free society is the autonomy it affords its members to strike the bargains of their choice, provided they do not harm others. Freedom of contract may be defended also on utilitarian grounds: by enforcing contracts in accordance with the value placed on things by the market, resources – goods and services – may be bought by those who place the highest value upon them. It is sometimes claimed that this yields a just distribution of scarce resources.

Those who champion the free market consider individuals to be the best judges of their welfare. In the 19th century – especially in England – the law of contract, as the facilitator of the optimum relations of exchange, was developed to a high degree of sophistication (some would say mystification) in pursuit of this cardinal value of commercial and industrial life. It is certainly true that business is unimaginable without rules of contract, but there is an inevitable inequality of bargaining power in any society. In theory, my contract with the electricity company that supplies power to my home regards both parties as being on an equal footing. But this is simply not the case. I am hardly in a position to haggle over the terms of the agreement which is inexorably a standard form contract. A featherweight is engaged in a contest with a squad of heavyweights. The law therefore tempers the hardship of so-called 'unfair' terms by consumer legislation and other institutional means that attempt to redress the balance by, for instance, empowering courts to disallow unconscionable clauses and permitting them to enforce only 'reasonable' terms.

In order to constitute a *binding* contract, the law normally requires that the parties to the agreement actually *intend* to create legal relations. Breaking a promise is almost always regarded as immoral, yet it results in legal consequences only where certain requirements are satisfied, though in certain civil law countries (such as France, Germany, and Holland) a person may be held liable – even before his offer is accepted – for failing to negotiate in good faith.

The common law notionally dissects agreement into an offer by one party and an acceptance of that offer by the other. By making an offer the 'offeror' expresses – by word, speech, fax, email, or even by conduct – his readiness to be bound in contract when it is accepted by the person to whom the offer is addressed, the 'offeree'. Thus Adam advertises his car for sale for $1,000. Eve offers him $600. Adam replies that he will accept $700. This is a counter-offer, which Eve is obviously free to accept or reject. Should she accept, there is agreement and, provided the other legal requirements are satisfied, a binding contract. This analysis is a helpful method by which to determine whether agreement has actually taken place, but it is rather artificial; it is often difficult to say who the offeror is and who the offeree is. For example, final agreement may be preceded by protracted negotiations involving numerous proposals and counter-proposals by the parties. To describe the process as constituting offer and acceptance is something of a fiction.

Hundreds of cases have grappled with factual situations that do not fit neatly into an offer-and-acceptance paradigm. There is also the recurring difficulty of the extent to which, if at all, an offeror should be bound by his offer. The common law stipulates that until you accept my offer I am at liberty to withdraw it. German, Swiss, Greek, Austrian, and Portuguese law, on the other hand, provide that I am bound by my offer; I cannot simply revoke it with impunity. A purported withdrawal has no legal effect. French and Italian law adopts an intermediate position. The Italian Civil Code provides that an offer may not be revoked before the expiry of a specified period. If no period is specified in the offer, it may be withdrawn until acceptance. But if the offeree has relied on the offer in good faith, he may claim damages for his loss in preparing to perform his side of the bargain.

The common law requires evidence not only of a serious intention to be legally bound, but also what is known as 'consideration', a concept absent from civil law systems. Consideration is the bargain element of the agreement: each party stands to gain something from the agreement – otherwise they would not have entered into it. These elements are illustrated by the classic case of *Carlill v Carbolic Smoke Ball Company* in 1892. The Carbolic Smoke Ball Company advertised its product – a smoke ball that it claimed would protect the user from contracting influenza. It undertook to pay £100 to anyone who, after using the apparatus, caught the 'flu. The advertisement included the following statement:

> £100 reward will be paid by the Carbolic Smoke Ball Company to any person who contracts the increasing epidemic influenza, colds or any disease caused by taking cold, after having used the ball three times daily for two weeks according to the printed directions

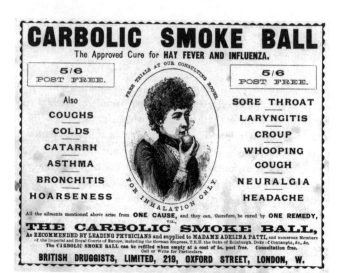

CARBOLIC SMOKE BALL

The Approved Cure for HAY FEVER AND INFLUENZA.

5/6 POST FREE.

5/6 POST FREE.

FREE TRIALS AT OUR CONSULTING ROOMS

Also
COUGHS
COLDS
CATARRH
ASTHMA
BRONCHITIS
HOARSENESS

SORE THROAT
LARYNGITIS
CROUP
WHOOPING COUGH
NEURALGIA
HEADACHE

FOR INHALATION ONLY.

All the ailments mentioned above arise from **ONE CAUSE**, and they can, therefore, be cured by **ONE REMEDY**, viz.,

THE CARBOLIC SMOKE BALL,

As **RECOMMENDED BY LEADING PHYSICIANS** and supplied to **MADAME ADELINA PATTI**, and numerous Members of the Imperial and Royal Courts of Europe, including the German Empress, T.R.H. the Dukes of Edinburgh, Duke of Connaught, &c., &c. The **CARBOLIC SMOKE BALL** can be refilled when empty at a cost of 5s. post free. Consultation free. Call or Write for Particulars.

BRITISH DRUGGISTS, LIMITED, 219, OXFORD STREET, LONDON, W.

5. **Despite the promises made by the company, Mrs Carlill, having bought and used the company's smoke ball according to the instructions, nevertheless contracted influenza. This legendary 19th-century English case established some of the fundamental conditions for the formation of a valid contract**

supplied with each ball. £1000 is deposited with the Alliance Bank, Regent Street, shewing our sincerity in the matter.

Mrs Carlill, relying on this promise, purchased a ball and used it according to the instructions. She nevertheless contracted influenza. The company claimed that there was no enforceable contract between it and Mrs Carlill since their offer had not been accepted – she had not informed the company that she had accepted its offer. Nor, they argued, was there any consideration because the company had not received any benefit from a purchaser's use of the smoke ball once it had been sold. Both arguments were rejected by the court. It held that the advertisement constituted an offer of a *unilateral* contract between the company and anyone who, having seen the advertisement, acted on it. (Normally, contracts are *bilateral*: they involve an exchange of promises between two parties.) In this case, however, since Mrs Carlill had satisfied the conditions, she was entitled to enforcement of the contract. Informing the company that she had used the ball formed part of the acceptance. Moreover, by depositing £1000 in the bank to 'show their sincerity in the matter' the company was plainly making a serious offer. In respect of consideration, the court ruled that Mrs Carlill's conduct constituted consideration for the promise to pay her the £100 reward.

Thus I agree to sell you my car; I stand to gain the purchase price and you, the ownership of the vehicle. If I ignore my agreement with you and sell my car to someone else, you may invoke the law to obtain a remedy – because you relied on my keeping my promise. This is known as breach of contract, which is discussed below.

In their general approach to contracts, there is unquestionably a divergence between the major systems of law. The common law is normally regarded as pragmatic and business-oriented, while the civil law tends to be more moralistic. It is nevertheless possible to postulate a number of general principles that are accepted, to a greater or lesser extent, by both legal systems.

It is usually the case that social agreements are not binding. As described above, our agreement to meet for a drink lacks the necessary intention to be bound in law. Nor will a court allow me to recover the expenses I incurred travelling to the bar where you promised you would be waiting for me. The common law, as we saw, requires also that, in return for a promise, the promisee must give 'consideration'. This may lead to absurd or unjust consequences. For example, in a famous English case, two sailors jumped ship. The captain was unable to replace them so he promised the rest of the crew more money, but reneged on his undertaking. The sailors lost their claim for the extra wages because they were already bound by their contract to assume extra duties on board. They had given no new consideration in return for the captain's promise to increase their pay. Various technical means have been devised by courts, especially in the United States, to avoid this sort of injustice.

The parties must have the capacity to enter into a contract. Though they differ in detail, all legal systems control the extent to which their members have the competence to enter into contractual relations. In particular, the young (minors) or those afflicted by mental or other impairments of their rational faculties are generally regarded as incapable of binding themselves contractually.

Contrary to the popular myth, a contract does not generally need to be in writing. Apart from certain contracts (the sale of land is the most conspicuous example), no formality is required to bind the parties. An oral agreement is generally no less binding than a written one, though, as we have seen, the common law requires evidence of consideration in return for a promise. Increasing government paternalism – in the name of consumer protection – has, however, generated a rise in the number of formalities, including written, or more usually, printed contracts required by legislation.

Certain 'contracts' are void because they offend 'public policy'. The concept of freedom of contract notwithstanding, the law will not countenance agreements that seek to use the law to achieve immoral or unlawful objectives. They are likely to be struck down by courts as void. But social mores rarely stand still; what was considered immoral a century ago appears tame in today's permissive circumstances. For example, German courts would once routinely negate a lease of premises for use as a brothel.

Mistake, misrepresentation, or duress may render a contract voidable. This is because there is, in effect, no genuine agreement.

Under certain circumstances, therefore, the law may allow me to void the contract where there has been a mistake, misrepresentation, duress, or undue influence. For example, if I am mistaken as to the subject of the contract (I thought I was buying a Ferrari, you were, in fact, selling a Ford), or you have misrepresented the Ford as a Ferrari, or you forced me into the sale, I have defences to your claim that I should perform my side of the agreement, and if I can show that there has been, say, fraudulent misrepresentation, the contract may be vitiated.

A court may award damages for breach of contract. Should I fail to perform my obligations under a contract, you may sue me to recover compensation or, in a limited number of cases, compel me to carry out my side of the bargain. If, however, I can show that circumstances have rendered performance impossible or that the purpose of the contract has been frustrated, I may escape liability for breach of contract. Suppose I agree to rent you my villa for a week. You arrive at the door and I refuse to allow you to enter. I appear to have breached our contract and you may want to obtain compensation. But how much? Should the law attempt to place you in the position you were in before you entered into the contract with me? Or should it seek to restore you to the position you would have been in if the contract had been carried out? Or should I simply be required to return the deposit I took from you in order to secure your booking? What if I refused you access to the villa because a storm had rendered the electricity supply unsafe? Would it make a difference if the storm occurred a month ago or only yesterday?

These thorny questions have spawned a plethora of intricate judicial analysis in all the major legal systems. The solutions differ, occasionally significantly, but typically where a party's breach is completely outside of his control – natural disasters offer the best example – he may be released from his contractual obligations.

Tort

Torts (or delicts, as they are called in Continental legal systems)
are civil wrongs; they include injuries to my person, property,
reputation, privacy, even my peace of mind. Like the law of
contract, the law of tort provides victims (or 'plaintiffs') with
the right to obtain compensation for their loss. Unlike contract,
however, which has as its principal goal the keeping of promises,
tort law protects a wide range of interests. The law provides
remedies, pre-emptive and compensatory, for conduct that causes
harm either intentionally or negligently. The latter have become
the principal focus of modern tort law. Accidents will happen,
but where they are the consequence of your negligence, I may be
able to recover damages to recompense my loss. So, for example,
should you run me over in your car, and I can prove that you were
driving negligently, I may be awarded damages to cover the cost of
my hospital treatment, the money I lost through being away from
work, and my pain and suffering.

To succeed, the plaintiff normally has to prove that the wrong was
done intentionally or negligently. Most torts are actionable only
when they have caused actual injury or damage, though certain
torts whose principal purpose is to protect rights rather than to
compensate for damage (such as trespass) are actionable without
proof of damage. The defendant (known also as the tortfeasor in
common law systems) is normally the person who is primarily
liable, though according to the rules of vicarious liability, one
person (e.g., an employer) may be held liable for a tort committed
by another person (e.g., an employee).

Torts are sometimes also breaches of contract. For example, the
negligent driver of a bus who causes injury to his passengers has
committed both the tort of negligence and a breach of the contract
to carry the passengers safely to their destinations. They may
recover damages either in tort or for breach of contract, or both.

The bus driver may also have committed a crime (e.g., dangerous driving).

While the protection of the interests in property and bodily security are reasonably straightforward, the courts of many jurisdictions have encountered difficulties when it comes to compensating victims whose loss is not physical, but either purely economic or emotional. Suppose, as occurred in an English case, the defendants negligently damage an electrical cable while carrying out construction work near the plaintiff's factory. As a result, the production is severely harmed and the plaintiff suffers financial loss. The physical loss (the damage to the materials) was clearly recoverable, but since the cable was not the plaintiff's property the loss was 'purely economic'. Can he recoup it? The common law, after some twists and turns by English courts, answers in the negative. The fear seems to be that allowing recovery will open the floodgates of litigation, a frequent concern expressed by judges, especially in England. In France, on the other hand, no distinction is drawn between physical and economic loss.

Comparable judicial trepidation attends the question of emotional distress. Where the injury consists of psychiatric illness as a result of physical harm, the courts look for some degree of 'proximity' between the plaintiff and the victim. The complexity of this calculation is tragically illustrated by a House of Lords decision in 1992. A crush in a sports stadium resulted in the death of 95 football fans, and more than 400 were injured. The police acknowledged their negligence in allowing too many spectators into an already overcrowded ground. The match was to have been televised live. In the event, vivid images of the disaster were broadcast. The disturbing pictures were seen by some of the plaintiffs who knew that their friends or family were present in the stadium. Two of the plaintiffs were spectators in the ground, but not in the stands where the disaster occurred; the other plaintiffs learned of the disaster through radio or television broadcasts. All the plaintiffs lost, or feared they might have lost, a relative or friend in the calamity. They failed in their claim for compensation for emotional distress because they did not satisfy one or other of the control mechanisms used by the law when damages for psychiatric injury are claimed by plaintiffs who were not directly threatened by the accident but learned of it through sight or hearing. These limiting factors are:

> 1. There must be a close tie of love and affection between the plaintiff and the victim. 2. The plaintiff must have been present at the accident or its immediate aftermath. 3. The psychiatric injury must have been caused by direct perception of the accident or its immediate aftermath and not by hearing about it from somebody else.

This requirement of 'proximity', as well as the other tests, have attracted considerable criticism, and calls for reform of the law in some jurisdictions. Problems also arise in circumstances where the injury falls short of a recognized mental affliction, and consists of the grief and distress that normally attends the loss of or injury to a loved one.

The law of tort not only attempts to recompense victims, it seeks also to deter persons from engaging in conduct that may injure others. Furthermore, it is said to 'shift' or 'distribute' the losses incurred in the case of negligent injury. To put the matter simply, where you are at fault in causing my injury, the law shifts the loss to you. Why should I have to bear the loss that you have negligently caused? You will see at once that this apparently facile question conceals a host of difficult issues about the nature of negligence: what is 'fault', what constitutes a 'cause', and so on. In the modern world dominated by insurance, the issue tends to alter from blame to burden: instead of asking 'who is at fault?' the question becomes 'who can best bear the cost?' And the answer is often the insurance company, with whom there is normally a compulsory liability insurance policy.

The common law of torts is a veritable cornucopia of wrongs, including trespass to land, trespass to person (which includes assault and battery), nuisance, defamation, breach of statutory duty, and strict liability. But, as mentioned, in practice they are eclipsed by the tort of negligence, which is based on the fault principle. The plaintiff must prove that the defendant owed him a *duty of care* which was breached by his failure to live up to the standard of '*the reasonable man*', thereby *causing* the plaintiff injury or damage.

Each of these three elements requires brief elaboration. The duty of care was vividly encapsulated in one of the most celebrated judicial pronouncements in all of the common law. In the landmark case of *Donoghue v Stevenson*, Mrs Donoghue complained of finding a snail in a ginger beer bottle, but the judgment was considerably more portentous. The precise facts of the case have never been clearly established, but it appears that Mrs Donoghue accompanied her friend to a café in the Scottish town of Paisley. Her friend ordered drinks. The café owner poured some of the contents of a bottle of ginger beer into a glass containing ice cream. Mrs Donoghue drank some of the contents and her friend lifted the bottle to pour the remainder of the ginger beer into the glass. Allegedly, a decomposed snail floated out of the bottle into the glass. Mrs Donoghue subsequently complained of stomach pain, and her doctor diagnosed her as having gastro-enteritis. She also claimed to have suffered emotional distress as a result of the incident. The law of tort did not then permit her to sue the café owner. Nevertheless, the House of Lords held that a plaintiff in the position of Mrs Donoghue was owed a duty of care by a manufacturer like Stevenson who had made the ginger beer. Drawing on the biblical injunction that one has a duty to love one's neighbour, Lord Atkin famously declared:

> The rule that you are to love your neighbour becomes in law you must not injure your neighbour; and the lawyer's question: Who is my neighbour? receives a restricted reply. You must take reasonable

care to avoid acts or omissions which you can reasonably foresee would be likely to injure your neighbour. Who, then, in law, is my neighbour? The answer seems to be – persons who are so closely and directly affected by my act that I ought reasonably to have them in contemplation as being so affected when I am directing my mind to the acts or omissions that are called in question.

In other words, you owe a duty to persons whom it is foreseeable are likely to be harmed by your conduct.

The standard of care is therefore an *objective* one: you are judged by reference to the reasonable man. Thus, for example, an English court held that the standard of care expected of a learner driver was the same as any other driver of a motor vehicle. Finally, as a matter of fact the defendant must cause the plaintiff's loss. The question of causation has exercised the mind of many a common law judge; concepts such as 'remoteness of damage' and 'proximate cause' seem frequently to obscure what is ultimately a policy decision by the court as to what it considers to be fair or in the best interests of society.

The reasonable man – the hypothetical person against whom a defendant's conduct is measured – is often described as 'the man

The reasonable man

[He is] devoid of any human weakness, with not one single saving vice, *sans* prejudice, procrastination, ill-nature, avarice, and absence of mind, as careful for his own safety as he is for that of others, this excellent but odious character stands like a monument in our courts of justice, vainly appealing to his fellow citizens to order their lives after his own example.

A. P. Herbert, *Uncommon Law* (Methuen, 1969), p. 4

on the Clapham omnibus', though in an examination, one of my students preferred 'the man on the clapped-out omnibus'.

A similar approach is evident in the equally legendary American case of *MacPherson v Buick Motor Co.* in which Justice Cardozo held that where a manufacturer negligently produces a defective car that injures the person who purchased it from the dealer, the manufacturer is liable to that person despite the absence of a contract between them and the person injured.

The plaintiff in a negligence action is required to prove that the defendant's conduct actually *caused* his injury or damage. It is often the case, however, that the relationship between cause and effect is too remote. This question has proved remarkably complex and has generated a vast body of case law, especially in England. It is not always clear whether in order to be held liable

---

The Learned Hand negligence formula

In 1947, Judge Learned Hand of the US Court of Appeals expounded the following algebraic solution to the question of how far a defendant needs to go to avoid an accident:

$$B < p \times L$$

B = the burden of precautions required to avoid the accident.

p = the probability that the accident will occur unless the precautions are taken.

L = the magnitude of the loss that will result if the accident occurs.

There is negligence when the actor's burden (B) is less than the probability (p) of harm, multiplied by the degree of loss (L). In other words, if the cost of the precautions is lower than the cost of the accident, the defendant is negligent.

---

the defendant must reasonably foresee the precise type of damage that results from his negligence. Nor is it certain that he will be held responsible for damage that is more extensive or that occurs in an atypical manner. The courts tend, on the whole, to decide these intractable cases on policy grounds.

To the plaintiff's claim that the defendant negligently caused his loss, the defendant may raise a number of defences, including that the plaintiff voluntarily accepted the risk by, say, accepting a lift from a seriously drunk driver. Or the defendant might argue that the plaintiff was himself negligent and therefore contributed to his injury by failing to notice that the driver was dangerously inebriated.

Certain special circumstances may, however, dictate that a defendant be held responsible regardless of whether he or she is at fault. This is known as 'strict liability'. The protection of public health or safety militates against the fault principle, especially where the defendant is engaged in an inherently dangerous activity such as the use of explosives. Liability is often perceived as the price to be paid in return for the profits made by large corporations that indulge in potentially harmful activities.

The French Civil Code is fairly sweeping in this respect. It imposes strict liability for the things 'which one has under one's control'. A 'thing' includes any corporeal object whether it consists of a gas, a fluid, electric cables, or radioactive materials. Motor vehicles are things. Italian law renders the driver of a vehicle strictly liable, unless he did everything possible to avoid the accident. The German law imposes strict liability on the driver of a vehicle who causes bodily injury or property damage, as well as on railway, gas, and electricity companies. The Anglo-American law finds the concept of strict liability less congenial, though under the so-called 'rule in *Rylands v Fletcher*' a defendant who brings onto his land a source of danger is strictly liable should it 'escape' and cause damage. The rule has been applied, amongst other hazards, to fire, gas, water, chemicals, fumes, electricity, and explosions. Strict liability may also arise under statute for harm caused by animals. An employer may also be held strictly liable for the acts of an employee in the course of his employment ('vicarious liability').

The difficulty of proving negligence by manufacturers has led to the considerable growth, especially in the United States, of a form of strict liability known as 'products liability'. The consumer is rarely able to check whether the car he buys is free of defects. The law therefore provides that if a product is defective at the time the defendant put it into circulation, the plaintiff need not prove negligence.

Product liabilty: the 'McDonald's Coffee Case'

This decision is frequently derided as an example of frivolous litigation that demeans the law of negligence. The facts may suggest otherwise.

A 79-year-old woman, Stella Liebeck, ordered a cup of coffee from a 'drive-through' McDonald's restaurant. She was in the passenger's seat. Her grandson parked the car in order that she could add cream and sugar to her coffee. She placed the coffee cup between her knees and pulled the far side of the lid towards her to remove it. In the process, she spilled the entire cup of coffee on her lap, causing her third-degree burns that required a skin graft and two years of follow-up treatment.

She sued McDonald's for gross negligence, claiming that they had sold coffee that was 'unreasonably dangerous' and 'defectively manufactured'. She adduced evidence that McDonald's required its restaurants to serve coffee at 82–88 degrees Celsius (which would cause a third-degree burn in 2 to 7 seconds), and argued that that the maximum temperature at which coffee should be served is 60 degrees

Celsius. McDonald's very hot coffee, it was claimed, could cause third-degree burns requiring a skin graft, in 12 to 15 seconds. McDonald's argued that it dispensed very hot coffee from its drive-through windows, because customers normally wanted to drive away with the coffee; the high temperature would ensure it stayed hot.

The evidence demonstrated that between 1982 and 1992 the company had received more than 700 complaints of customers being burned by hot coffee. It had settled claims arising from scalding injuries for more than $500,000, or one complaint per 24 million cups of coffee bought.

The jury found McDonald's 80% liable for the incident and Mrs Liebeck, 20% liable. The coffee cup contained a warning, but the jury decided that it was inadequate. It awarded her damages of US$200,000, which was subsequently reduced by 20% to $160,000. In addition, the jury awarded her $2.7 million in punitive damages (to punish McDonald's). This latter sum was reduced by the judge to $480,000. She thus received a total of $640,000. The decision was appealed by both parties, but the case was eventually settled out of court for an undisclosed amount under $600,000.

Another recent, predominantly American, development is the emergence of so-called 'mass torts'. These are lawsuits launched by a large number of plaintiffs ('class actions') associated with a single product. They include product liability claims against, for example, tobacco companies, for lung cancer caused by smoking, injuries caused by breast implants, and large-scale, 'man-made' disasters, such as aeroplane crashes and explosions at chemical plants.

The cost, delays, and injustices of the fault principle have generated deep dissatisfaction with the tort system of compensating accident victims. This has become so widespread and pervasive that cynicism greets the attempts by the rapidly declining number of fault-based stalwarts who attempt to defend its continuation. The only members of society who profit from the system, it is charged, are the lawyers. Some jurisdictions (notably New Zealand and Quebec) have introduced comprehensive systems of no-fault insurance under which the law of tort is abolished for personal injury caused by accident. Victims of accidents are compensated from special funds created for this purpose. Detractors question the consequence of this munificence on the deterrent effect of a fault-based system, though it is widely acknowledged that, especially in the case of traffic accidents, compulsory insurance policies are the death knell of tort law.

In addition to wrongs committed negligently, the law recognizes a number of intentional torts or delicts. Among them is the civil wrong of defamation. The classic (rather technical) definition of the common law tort of defamation is that the wrong consists in publishing a false statement about the plaintiff which tends to lower him or her in the estimation of right-thinking members of the community generally, or which tends to cause him or her to be shunned or avoided, or which bring him or her into hatred, ridicule, or contempt, or which tend to discredit him or her in his or her trade or profession.

The test is an objective one; the fact that the defendant did not intend to defame the plaintiff is not a relevant consideration. Nor does it matter that he was unaware of the circumstances which rendered an apparently innocuous statement defamatory, or that the statement is not believed to be true by anyone who reads it. The defendant may be held liable for the repetition of defamatory statements where he authorizes or intends such repetition, but, as a general rule, he is not liable for unauthorized repetition unless the person to whom it was published was under a duty to repeat it. Therefore in the case of a book, several publications normally occur: the author to the publisher; the author and publisher jointly to the printer; by the author, publisher, and printer jointly to the distributor; and so on. Each repetition is a new publication which gives rise to a new course of action. The law does, however, distinguish between those who are mere distributors, on the one hand, and those who take an active part in the production of the work, on the other. Similar questions may arise in respect of the publishing of a libel on the Internet.

There are four main defences to an action for defamation. First is the defence of justification (or 'truth'). Acknowledging the significance of free speech, the law provides that it is a complete answer to an action for defamation for the defendant to prove that the statement he published is substantially true. Second, the defence of absolute privilege protects defamatory statements when made in the course of legislative, judicial, and other official proceedings. Third, the defence of qualified privilege obtains in circumstances where the defendant has a duty (legal, social, or moral) to make a statement to a person who has a corresponding interest or duty to receive it, i.e., where the publisher and those to whom the publication is made have a common interest in the data concerned. The defence extends to fair and accurate reports of legislative and judicial proceedings. Fourth, there is the defence of fair comment which, in practice, tends to be the most important. This defence protects honest expressions of opinion on matters of public interest and is particularly relevant to the protection of free speech – a fact recognized by the courts. The comment must be on a matter of public interest. Matters of public interest have been held to include the public conduct of persons who hold or seek a public office or position of public trust, the administration of justice, political and state matters, the management of public institutions, works of art, public performances, and anything that invites comment or challenges public attention. But the statement must be one of opinion not fact. This is a distinction that is easier to draw in theory than in practice. It must be 'fair', that is, it must be based on facts, and supported by those facts; there must be a basis of fact sufficient to warrant the comment made. The facts upon which the comment is based must be true. If they are true and the defendant is honestly expressing his genuine opinion on a subject of public interest, then it does not matter whether a reasonable person would hold such an opinion.

The plaintiff may defeat the defence by proving that the defendant was actuated by malice. It is for the plaintiff to prove malice. Malice defeats also the defence of qualified privilege. In respect of fair comment, malice denotes any improper motive which may have caused the defendant to make his comment. In this sense, then, his comment is not an honest expression of his view. As a general rule, the test is 'Did the defendant believe the statement to be true?'

Rather than recognizing a separate tort of defamation, civil law systems protect reputation under the wing of personality rights. In several respects, the approach in Germany, France, and other European countries is more stringent than the common law. For example, the defences such as fair comment and justification are often not available. The free speech provisions of the European Convention on Human Rights, however, have tempered the harshness of the law. Most European countries protect the plaintiff also against 'insults', a potentially unlimited area of liability that has been criticized by the European Court of Human Rights. On the other hand, while awards of damages tend in common law courts to be high (sometimes exceptionally so), the fines imposed by European courts are relatively trifling.

Criminal law

Crime is irresistible – and not only to criminals. It is the stuff of popular culture. Think of the numerous – mostly American – movies such as *The Godfather*, *Taxi Driver*, *Pulp Fiction*, *Scarface*, *Reservoir Dogs*, and countless others, or the many popular television series portraying various aspects of crime and its detection, including *Law and Order*, *NYPD Blue*, *Hill Street Blues*, *The Sopranos*, to name only a few. We seem to revel in observing the criminal process unfold.

Typically the criminal law punishes serious forms of antisocial behaviour: murder, theft, rape, blackmail, robbery, assault, and battery. Yet governments deploy the law to criminalize a host of minor forms of misbehaviour relating, in particular, to health and safety. These 'regulatory offences' occupy a sizeable proportion of modern criminal law. As with the law of tort, the concept of fault is central to the criminal law. Broadly speaking, most countries proscribe conduct that generates insecurity, causes offence, and harms the efficient operation of the government, the economy, or society in general.

Virtually every system of criminal law requires evidence of fault – intention or negligence – to convict a person of an offence. So, for example, the American Model Penal Code defines a crime as 'conduct that unjustifiably and inexcusably inflicts or threatens substantial harm to individual or public interests'. Criminal liability thus has three basic components: conduct, without justification and without excuse. To amount to a crime, 'conduct' must inflict or threaten substantial harm to individual or public interests. In sum, therefore, criminal liability requires a person to engage in conduct that inflicts or threatens substantial harm to individual or public interests without justification and without excuse.

The criterion of 'harm' will differ according to the social and political values of each society, but all agree that conduct that impairs the security of the community or hurts the physical well-being or welfare of its members constitutes 'harm'.

Criminal responsibility normally entails the presence of a guilty act (the '*actus reus*') as well as a guilty mind ('*mens rea*'). But

these prerequisites will not ineluctably condemn the accused,
for he may have one of several defences to excuse his otherwise
criminal behaviour. Suppose I am attacked by a knife-wielding
robber, and in the affray that ensues I slay my assailant. Provided
I use 'reasonable force' to defend myself, I am entitled to a
complete acquittal. The defence is, however, unlikely to excuse
me killing to defend my property. Other defences include duress
(where, for example, I am forced at the point of a gun to commit
a crime), mistake (I genuinely believed the umbrella I took was
mine), incapacity (the defendant is a child, too young to form the
requisite *mens rea*), provocation, and insanity.

The traditional offences mentioned above are everywhere crimes,
albeit they are met with varying degrees of severity or form of
punishment. In addition, society cannot tolerate attacks upon its
own survival; treason, terrorism, and public disorder are therefore
generally criminalized. Nor is the criminal law confined to these
extreme assaults on the community; conduct that offends may
attract the attention of the law where the affront or nuisance
is sufficient: public nudity, excessive noise or odours, and
prostitution are examples of conduct that may cross the threshold.
And there is a tendency for criminal law to be utilized in pursuit
of paternalistic ends. Think, for example, of laws requiring the
wearing of seat belts or crash helmets, or the legislation of most
countries prohibiting the possession of drugs. The ostensible
purpose of these laws is to protect individuals against their own
folly or fragility.

The common law requires that in order to convict the defendant
his guilt must be proved 'beyond reasonable doubt'. Civil cases
(such as an action for breach of contract or a tortious action for
damages) relax the burden to one of 'a balance of probabilities'.
The situation in respect of criminal trials in civilian legal systems
is broadly the same, though the so-called 'inquisitorial' system
obtaining in Continental Europe and other civil jurisdictions is
often misunderstood, and the differences exaggerated.

As in tort, liability in the criminal law is occasionally strict, i.e., there are offences that can be committed without *mens rea*. Similarly, the rationale for this abandonment of fault is the protection of public welfare, for example, where a factory is held responsible for industrial pollution – despite the absence of negligence.

The prosecution must, of course, prove that the defendant did actually commit the offence with which he has been charged. Suppose we have a fight and I hit you on the head with a blunt instrument. You are rushed to hospital, where you are administered a drug that kills you. Am I guilty of your murder? Did I *cause* your death? Were it not for the wound I inflicted, you would not have been in the hospital that negligently administered the incorrect medication. But it is doubtful that any legal system would hold me responsible for your death.

Murder in most countries requires proof of the intention to kill ('malice aforethought' in the common law). Legal systems attempt, in a variety of ways, to classify homicide on the basis of the mental element involved. So, for example, the United States and Canada tend to distinguish between different types of killing that constitute murder. Thus, according to the Canadian Criminal Code, first-degree murder is the intentional, premeditated killing of another person or in the furtherance of another serious criminal offence such as robbery. Second-degree murder is the intentional killing of another person without premeditation (i.e. killing in the heat of the moment). Thirdly, there is manslaughter, which is the killing of another person when there is no intent to kill. Fourth is infanticide – the killing of an infant while the mother is still recovering from the birth.

While liability for intentional killing is relatively uncontroversial, death caused by negligence is less straightforward, and the laws of various jurisdictions adopt different solutions to what is generally regarded as something of a quandary. Some require that the defendant *must have known* – subjectively – that his act may kill someone and that he nevertheless proceeds recklessly despite the risk. For example, I have been admonished never to point a loaded weapon at anyone. I ignore the warning, and the rifle I point towards you fires and you are killed. Other jurisdictions lack this prerequisite of knowledge and impose liability for negligent killing where the defendant acts with gross negligence. Still others require only ordinary negligence.

One of the primary functions of the criminal law is to authorize the punishment of convicted offenders. This may be justified on any of a number of (often competing) grounds. First, punishment is thought, sometimes correctly, to act as a deterrent both to the convict and to others. Few criminals, however, imagine they will be apprehended; the effectiveness of deterrence is thus questionable. Second, there are those who believe that through punishment, especially imprisonment, the offender will come to see the error of his ways and emerge a reformed individual. Unhappily, the evidence in support of this benevolent attitude is meagre. It is argued, third, that the real purpose of punishment is retribution or desert: making the wrongdoer suffer for his crime: 'an eye for an eye ...'. An extreme example is Islamic *Sharia* law, under which, according to most interpretations, the punishment for serious theft is the amputation of hands or feet (though for first offenders only one hand is cut off).

The state, by assuming responsibility for chastising the criminal, reduces the risk of victims of crime 'taking the law into their own hands'. Fourth, by locking up an offender, he is removed from society, thereby protecting the rest of us. Finally, especially in the case of minor offences, the criminal may be required to make amends through 'community service'. This form of punishment is then justified as a form of 'restorative justice'.

Property

Ownership is at the epicentre of social organization. The manner in which the law defines and protects this exclusive right is an important marker of the nature of society. And the law always has something to say on this subject, whether it is to confer absolute rights of private property, recognize collective rights, or adopt a position in between. Specifically, the law of property determines, first, what counts as 'property'; second, when a person acquires an exclusive right to a thing; and, third, the manner in which it protects this right.

To the first question there is general agreement that property includes land, buildings, and goods. The common law distinguishes between real property (land as distinct from personal or movable possessions) and personal property. Civil law systems distinguish between movable and immovable property. The former corresponds roughly to personal property, while immovable property corresponds to real property. But property is what the law declares it to be: a ten dollar bill is a piece of paper with no intrinsic value; the law imparts value to it. In a similar fashion, the law may create property, as it does in the case of intellectual property (which includes copyright). As the owner of the copyright in this book, I have a monopoly of various rights over its copying and reproduction.

The second issue, who is the owner, is generally determined by discovering who has the strongest long-term right to control the thing in question. And this right will normally include the right to transfer ownership to another. In the case of land, however, I may not know whether the seller is the legal owner. Most legal systems therefore have some form of public land registration which enables prospective buyers to establish who the genuine owner is.

Third, the law may be called upon to settle a contest between the owner and the possessor of a thing. The former is, as we have seen, the person with the strongest long-term claim to the possession of a thing. But suppose I rent my villa to you for a year. You currently possess the property, and while I have an ultimate right to possess it, some legal systems favour the right of the tenant (at least for the duration of the lease) over the owner; others prefer the owner.

A significant branch of property law is the law of trusts, which developed out of the division in England between common law and equity. In the 14th century, dissatisfaction with the rigidity, corruption, and formalism of the common law led losing parties to petition the king to compel the other party to observe moral – rather than strictly legal – principles. The king conveyed these petitions to the chancellor, the chief administrative official, who, in time, came to adopt judicial powers, and the idea of equity was born. The inexorable conflict between the strict application of the law, on the one hand, and the principles of justice and morality, was well understood by Shakespeare who, in Act IV Scene 1 of *The Merchant of Venice*, has Portia declare:

> The quality of mercy is not strained
> It droppeth as the gentle rain from heaven
> Upon the place beneath. It is twice blest;
> It blesseth him that gives and him that takes.
> 'Tis mightiest in the mightiest; it becomes
> The thronèd monarch better than his crown.

Among the concepts to emerge from this equitable jurisdiction was the convenient institution of the trust, which is an arrangement by which a 'settlor' transfers property to one or more trustees who hold it for the benefit of one or more beneficiaries who have the right to enforce the trust in court.

Equity, rooted in conscience, spawned also a number of important remedies, including the injunction. This enables a person to prevent in advance the commission of a legal wrong. For example, if I learn that you are about to publish an article defamatory of

6. Disguised as a young doctor of law, Shakespeare's Portia in *The Merchant of Venice* successfully persuaded the court that, while Shylock was indeed entitled to his pound of Antonio's flesh, he was legally required to remove it without shedding any blood! This nice legal technicality saved Antonio's life

> ### The Dickensian Court of Chancery
>
> This is the Court of Chancery, which has its decaying houses
> and its blighted lands in every shire, which has its worn-out
> lunatic in every madhouse and its dead in every churchyard,
> which has its ruined suitor with his slipshod heels and
> threadbare dress borrowing and begging through the round
> of every man's acquaintance, which gives to monied might
> the means abundantly of wearying out the right, which so
> exhausts finances, patience, courage, hope, so overthrows the
> brain and breaks the heart, that there is not an honourable
> man among its practitioners who would not give – who does
> not often give – the warning, 'Suffer any wrong that can be
> done you rather than come here!'
>
> Charles Dickens, *Bleak House*, Chapter I

me, I may, in several jurisdictions, obtain an urgent injunction
to stop you from doing so. Another equitable remedy is 'specific
performance'. The common law allowed only the award of
damages for breach of contract, but often the plaintiff seeks the
performance of the contract rather than compensation. Since the
19th century, equity is applied in the same courts as the common
law, and though the division between the two bodies of law
lingers, equity has lost its mission as the 'compassionate female' in
contrast to the common law's position as the 'inflexible male'.

Constitutional and administrative law

Whether or not it is in written form, every country has a
constitution that specifies the composition and functions of the
organs of government, and regulates the relationship between
individuals and the state. Constitutional law analyses the extent
to which the functions of government are distributed between the
legislative, executive, and judicial branches of government: the

'separation of powers'. Many constitutions incorporate a bill of rights that constrains the exercise of the power of government by conferring individual rights and freedoms on citizens. Such rights typically include freedom of speech, conscience, religion, the right of peaceful assembly, freedom of association, the right of privacy, equality before and equal protection of law, the right to life, the right to marry and found a family, freedom of movement, and the rights of persons charged with or convicted of a criminal offence.

Administrative law governs the exercise of the powers and duties by public officials. In particular, it concerns the control of such powers by the courts who, in many jurisdictions, increasingly engage in reviewing the exercise of legislation and administrative action. This has occurred largely as a consequence of the dramatic expansion over the last 50 years in the number of government agencies that regulate vast tracts of our social and economic lives. It concerns also the review of decisions made by so-called 'quasi-judicial' bodies, like professional disciplinary committees that affect the legal rights of their members. Their rulings are susceptible to 'judicial review' to determine whether they have acted reasonably.

The precise standard of reasonableness to be applied by the court differs in various common law jurisdictions. In the United States, for example, the court asks whether the body's decision was 'arbitrary or capricious' before deciding whether to strike it down. The Canadian test is one of 'patent unreasonableness', while the Supreme Court of India deploys criteria of proportionality and legitimate expectation. English law adopts the standard known as '*Wednesbury* unreasonableness' (after a case of this name, in which it was held that a decision would be set aside if it 'is so unreasonable that no reasonable authority could ever have come to it').

In France, the *Conseil Constitutionel* exercises exclusive judicial oversight, including in respect of legislation that fails to attract sufficient parliamentary support. It has the – unappealable – power to nullify the contested bill. The supreme courts (*Conseil d'état* and *Cour de Cassation*) seek to interpret the law in a manner consistent with the Constitution. French administrative law recognizes certain '*principes à valeur constitutionnelle*' (principles of constitutional value), including human dignity, with which the executive must comply, even in the absence of specific legislative provisions to that effect. The German constitution (the Basic Law) guarantees judicial review as a check on the tyranny of the majority.

Several civil law countries have special administrative courts. Difficulties tend to arise in respect of determining whether a matter is one for these courts or belongs more properly in the ordinary courts. In France, for example, a special Tribunal of Conflicts decides where the matter should be heard, while in Germany the court in which the case is first pleaded determines whether it has jurisdiction and may transfer cases over which it denies jurisdiction. In Italy, the Court of Cassation is the ultimate authority when such conflicts arise.

Other branches

Family law relates to marriage (and its contemporary equivalents), divorce, children, child support, adoption, custody, guardianship, surrogacy, and domestic violence.

Public international law seeks to regulate the relations between sovereign states. These norms are generated by treaties and international agreements (such as the Geneva Conventions), the United Nations, and other international organizations, including the International Labour Organization, UNESCO, the World Trade Organization, and the International Monetary Fund. The International Court of Justice (sometimes called the World Court), based in The Hague, was established in 1945 under the UN Charter in order to settle legal disputes between states and to issue advisory opinions on legal matters. The International Criminal Court was established in 2002 and also sits at The Hague. It hears prosecutions of alleged perpetrators of genocide, crimes against humanity, war crimes, and the crime of aggression. More than 100 states are members of the court, but neither China nor the United States are among them; the latter expressing reservations about the ability of the court to respect the constitutional rights of American defendants (including trial by jury) and the prospect of the politicization of the court – fears that seem tenuous, and have not troubled the numerous nations that have recognized the court's jurisdiction.

Environmental law is a patchwork of common law rules, legislation, and international agreements and conventions whose chief concern is to protect the natural environment against the depredations of humans, such as carbon emissions that cause pollution and probably global warming. It seeks also to promote 'sustainable development'.

Company law deals with the 'floating' of corporations and other business organizations. The concept of 'corporate personality' (under which a company has a distinct identity independent of its members) is of vital importance in the business world. It means that a company is a legal person with the capacity to enter into contracts, sue and be sued. Company law stipulates also the rights and duties of directors and shareholders, and is increasingly concerned with rules of corporate governance, mergers, and acquisitions.

Chapter 3
Law and morality

Is homosexuality sinful? What's wrong with abortion? Why is racism bad? Moral questions of this kind arise inexorably in almost any legal system. And confronting them is among the fundamental characteristics of a free society. Moreover, the language of morals is increasingly employed on the international stage. When an American president described an 'axis of evil' existing between certain nations, he was (probably unconsciously) presuming a normative yardstick by which to measure the conduct of states, that, since the formation of the United Nations, is partly embodied in an expanding anthology of international declarations and conventions.

Although we cannot easily evade moral question marks, the identification, or even the acknowledgement, of moral values by which to live, is always contentious. Being or doing good is not necessarily synonymous with obeying the law, even though the law, its ideas and its institutions, are often informed by moral values. It would be strange if it were otherwise.

The relationship between the law and the moral practices (or 'positive morality') adopted by society may be represented by two partially intersecting circles. Where they overlap we find a correspondence between the law and moral values (for example, murder is both morally and legally prohibited in all societies).

Outside the overlapping zone, reside, on the one hand, acts which are legally wrong, but not necessarily immoral (for example, exceeding your time on a parking meter) and, on the other, conduct which is immoral, but not necessarily unlawful (such as adultery). The greater the intersection, the more likely the law is to be accepted and respected by members of that society.

In some cases, of course, there will be a conflict between the law and the moral code of certain individuals or groups. So, for example, a pacifist who is required to serve in the military may be compelled to become a conscientious objector and face imprisonment as a consequence of his violation of the law. Similarly, journalists in many countries claim a right not to disclose their sources. This will not, however, assist them when they are required to reveal this information as a witness in a trial.

More extreme is the situation in which the law actually conflicts with the majority's moral values. In apartheid South Africa, for instance, the law was used to pursue *immoral* aims. As the creation of a white minority, the political system disenfranchised every black person, and the law discriminated against them in several important aspects of social and economic life. In such cases, we may beg to ask whether unjust legislation of this kind qualifies as 'law'. Must law be moral? Can anything count as law?

A celebrated, if somewhat inconclusive, debate between two leading legal philosophers sought to establish the grounds, if any, upon which immoral laws may nevertheless be regarded as 'law'. At its heart was a decision of a post-war West German court. In 1944, during Nazi rule, a woman who wished to dispose of her husband denounced him to the Gestapo for insulting remarks he had made about Hitler's conduct of the war. The husband was tried and sentenced to death, though his sentence was converted to service as a soldier on the Russian front. After the war the wife was prosecuted for procuring her husband's loss of liberty. Her defence was that he had committed an offence under a Nazi statute of 1934. The court nevertheless convicted her on the ground that the statute under which the husband had been punished offended the 'sound conscience and sense of justice of all decent human beings'.

Professor H. L. A. Hart, Professor of Jurisprudence at Oxford, contended that the decision of the court, and similar cases pursuant to it, was wrong, because the Nazi law of 1934 was a formally valid law. Professor Lon Fuller of Harvard Law School, on the other hand, argued that, since Nazi 'law' deviated so significantly from morality, it failed to qualify as law. He therefore defended the court's decision, though both jurists express their preference for the enactment of retroactive legislation under which the woman could have been prosecuted.

For Fuller, law has an 'internal morality'. In his view, a legal system is the purposive human 'enterprise of subjecting human conduct to the guidance and control of general rules'. A legal system must conform to certain procedural standards, or what may appear to be a legal system is simply the bare exercise of state coercion. This 'inner morality of law' consists of eight essential principles, failure to comply with any one of them, or substantial failure in respect of several, suggests that 'law' does not exist in that society. He relates the sad tale of a king, Rex, who, to his cost, neglects these eight principles. He fails to make rules at all, deciding questions ad hoc. He fails also to publicize the rules. He enacts rules which are retroactive, difficult to understand, contradictory, and which require conduct beyond the powers of the affected party. Moreover, his rules change so frequently that the subject cannot adjust his action by them. Finally, there is no correspondence between the rules as announced and their actual administration.

These failures are, Fuller explains, mirrored by eight forms of 'legal excellence' towards which a system of rules may

aspire, and which are embodied in the 'inner morality of law'.
They are generality, promulgation, non-retroactivity, clarity,
non-contradiction, possibility of compliance, constancy,
congruence between declared rule and official action.

Where a system does not conform to any one of these principles,
or fails substantially in respect of several, it could not be said
that 'law' existed in that community. Thus, instead of adopting a
substantive natural law approach, Fuller espouses a procedural
natural law approach. The 'internal morality of law' is essentially
a 'morality of aspiration'. Nor does it claim to accomplish any
substantive ends, apart from the excellence of the law itself.

Not the law's business?

Professor Hart engaged in another important debate on the
relationship between law and morality. This time his adversary
was the English judge Lord Devlin. The so-called Hart/Devlin
debate illuminates certain fundamental aspects of the role of the
law in seeking to enforce morality. It is a classic confrontation
that remains the starting point for any serious discussion of this
subject, not only in Britain but throughout the world.

The catalyst for the debate was a report in 1957 by a British
committee, under the chairmanship of Sir John Wolfenden,
appointed to examine the question of homosexual offences and
prostitution. It concluded that the function of the criminal law
was to preserve public order and decency, to protect citizens
from what is offensive and injurious, and from exploitation
and corruption of others, especially those who are especially
vulnerable: the young, the inexperienced, and the frail. But:

> Unless a deliberate attempt is to be made by society, acting through
> the agency of the law, to equate the sphere of crime with that of
> sin, there must remain a realm of private morality and immorality
> which is, in brief and crude terms, not the law's business.

7. A child prodigy (he read Latin and Greek at the age of 8), John Stuart Mill's *On Liberty* is a classic exposition of the concept of freedom, especially in regard to the limits of state power over the individual. His 'harm principle' continues to animate debates on the proper reaches of the criminal law in a free society

In arriving at this conclusion (and recommending that both consensual homosexual acts between adults in private, and prostitution, should be decriminalized), the Wolfenden Committee was strongly influenced by the views of the 19th-century liberal utilitarian John Stuart Mill, who, in 1859, argued that:

> [T]he sole end for which mankind are warranted, individually or collectively, in interfering with the liberty of action of any of their number, is self-protection. The only purpose for which power can be rightfully exercised over any member of a civilized community, against his will, is to prevent harm to others. His own good, either physical or moral, is not a sufficient warrant.

At first blush, this 'harm principle' as the touchstone by which to fix the boundaries of the criminal law seems uncomplicated and attractive. But two immediate difficulties arise. First, is the criminal law not justified in punishing what another Victorian utilitarian, Sir James Fitzjames Stephen (uncle of the novelist Virginia Woolf), called 'the grosser forms of vice'? And, second, who is to say what constitutes 'harm'?

This pair of problems is the nucleus of the disagreement between Hart and Devlin. In a series of lectures in 1959, Lord Devlin took issue with the Wolfenden Committee's position, arguing that society has every right to punish conduct that, in the view of the ordinary member of society ('the man in the jury box'), is grossly immoral. Harm, he contended, is irrelevant; the fabric of society is maintained by a shared morality. This social cohesion is undermined when immoral acts are committed – even in private, and even if they harm no one. Societies disintegrate from within, he contended, more often than they are destroyed by external forces:

> There is disintegration when no common morality is observed and history shows that the loosening of moral bonds is often the

first stage of disintegration, so that society is justified in taking the same steps to preserve its moral code as it does to preserve its government ... [T]he suppression of vice is as much the law's business as the suppression of subversive activities.

But, though Lord Devlin concedes that only those acts that cause 'intolerance, indignation and disgust' warrant punishment, Professor Hart challenges the very foundation of his 'social cohesion' argument. Surely, Hart insists, a society does not require a shared morality; pluralistic, multicultural societies may contain a variety of moral views. Nor, even if there is a shared morality, is it obvious that its protection is essential to the survival of society. In respect of the first assertion, it does seem far-fetched to claim that a society's foundation is unable to withstand the challenge of a competing ideology or morality. Is a Western society gravely wounded by the Islamic prohibition of alcohol espoused by a significant proportion of its inhabitants? Equally, is an Islamic society unable to withstand the morality of a minority in its midst?

Hart does not, however, shrink from supporting a paternalistic role for the law. Differing with Mill, he acknowledges that there may be circumstances in which the law ought to protect individuals from physically harming themselves. The criminal law may therefore justifiably withhold the defence of consent to homicide and assault. Requiring seat belts in vehicles or crash helmets to be used by motorcyclists is a legitimate exercise of legal control.

A key distinction is also drawn by Hart between harm that is caused by public spectacle, on the one hand, and offence caused merely through knowledge, on the other. Hence bigamy may justifiably be punished since, as a public act, it may cause offence to religious sensitivities, whereas private consensual sexual acts by adults may cause offence – but only through knowledge, and thus do not justify punishment. Such acts are best dealt with by legislation. In the words of the distinguished English judge Lord Atkin:

> Notoriously there are wide differences of opinion today as to how far the law ought to punish immoral acts which are not done in the face of the public. Some think that the law already goes too far, some that it does not go far enough. Parliament is the proper place, and I am firmly of opinion the only proper place, to settle that. When there is sufficient support from public opinion, Parliament does not hesitate to intervene. Where Parliament fears to tread it is not for the courts to rush in.

A similar approach may be required in respect of the following matter.

A right to life?

Moral questions rarely admit of simple solutions. They frequently polarize society. The abortion debate in the United States is a compelling example. Christian groups condemn (occasionally violently) the practice of abortion, regarding it as murder of a foetus. Feminists, on the other hand, consider the matter as fundamental to a woman's right to control her own body. There is no apparent middle ground. Ronald Dworkin vividly portrays the ferocity of the struggle:

> The war between anti-abortion groups and their opponents is America's new version of the terrible seventeenth-century European civil wars of religion. Opposing armies march down streets or pack themselves into protests at abortion clinics, courthouses, and the White House, screaming at and spitting on and loathing one another. Abortion is tearing America apart.

At the core of the divisive subject of abortion is the decision of the United States Supreme Court in 1973 of *Roe v Wade* in which the court held, by a majority, that the abortion law of Texas was

8. The United States Supreme Court 1973 landmark decision in *Roe v Wade* continues to excite divisive, often acrimonious, debate. The court's ruling that laws against abortion violated the constitutional right to privacy is generally defended by feminist groups, and contested by pro-life advocates

unconstitutional as a violation of the right to privacy. Under that law abortion was criminalized, except when performed to save the pregnant woman's life. The court held that states may prohibit abortion to protect the life of the foetus only in the third trimester. The decision, which has been described as 'undoubtedly the best-known case the United States Supreme Court has ever decided' is simultaneously embraced by feminists, and denounced by many Christians. It is the – always vulnerable – slender thread by which the right of American women to a lawful abortion hangs.

In the abortion debate the sanctity of human life has somehow to be morally weighed against the right of a woman over her body. Most European countries have sought to strike this balance by legislation that permits abortion within specified periods under certain prescribed conditions. In Britain, for example, abortion is lawful if it is certified by two medical practitioners that to continue the pregnancy would involve risk to the life of, or injury to, the pregnant woman or her existing children, and that the risk is greater than if the pregnancy were terminated. It is lawful also if there is a substantial risk that if the child were born it would suffer serious physical or mental handicap. It is a criminal offence to terminate a pregnancy when the child is capable of being born alive. This is normally after 28 weeks. More recent legislation provides that a pregnancy that has not exceeded 24 weeks may be terminated where its continuation would involve risk, greater than if the pregnancy were terminated, of injury to the physical or mental health of the pregnant woman or any existing children of her family, but no time limit is imposed where termination may be necessary to prevent grave permanent injury to the physical or mental health of the pregnant woman, or risk to her life, or if there is a substantial risk that if the child were born it would suffer from such physical or mental abnormalities as to be seriously handicapped.

In its quest for a conscientious resolution to this complex issue, each society must appraise its own moral currency. If, as most humans tend to believe, life is sacred, does a foetus count as a person capable of suffering harm? If it does, how is ending its life to be distinguished from the humane killing of a living human? Should the welfare of the as yet unborn prevail over the distress suffered by a woman compelled to bear an unwanted pregnancy or endure the anxiety, cost, and difficulty of bringing up a handicapped child?

Comparable deliberation inevitably attends the equally daunting issue of euthanasia. Doctors, lawyers, and ultimately courts perennially wrestle with the contentious question of an individual's 'right to die'. A distinction is usually drawn (not always convincingly) between active and passive euthanasia. The former entails the acceleration of a person's life by a positive act, such as an injection of potassium chloride. Most legal systems treat this as murder. The latter involves the shortening of life by an omission to act: a withdrawal of treatment, which is increasingly accepted by both the law and the medical profession in many jurisdictions as humane. But courts have not always found it easy to determine the lawfulness of withdrawing life support from an incurably or terminally ill patient who is in a persistent vegetative state (PVS), unable to make an autonomous decision.

Nor are generalizations easy in respect of either the morality or lawfulness of ending the life of a patient. There is, for instance, an important distinction between a patient who is incurable, and one who is terminally ill. The latter spectrum may range between incapacity (a fully conscious patient who can breathe unaided), artificial support (a fully conscious patient attached to a ventilator), unconsciousness, to intensive care (where the patient is comatose and is attached to a ventilator). Different considerations arise in each of these situations.

The complexities provoked when the law encounters thorny moral questions of this kind suggest that they are not susceptible to resolution by slogans. 'The right to die', 'autonomy', 'self-determination', or 'the sanctity of life' are generously deployed in these debates, but the law must develop careful, reflective answers that best serve the public interest. Judges may not be the most appropriate arbiters, but is there an alternative? Two decisions of the courts (one English, one American) illustrate the perplexity involved.

The English case arose out of a crush that occurred at a football stadium in 1989 (see page 45). Anthony Bland sustained hypoxic brain damage which left him in a persistent vegetative state. Though his brain stem continued to function, his cerebral cortex (the seat of consciousness, communicative activity, and voluntary movement) was destroyed through lack of oxygen, but he was not 'legally dead'. The judge, Lord Justice Hoffmann (as he then was), described his wretched state as follows:

> He lies in ... hospital ... fed liquid food by a pump through a tube passing through his nose and down the back of his throat into his stomach. His bladder is emptied through a catheter inserted through his penis, which from time to time has caused infections requiring dressing and antibiotic treatment. His stiffened joints have caused his limbs to be rigidly contracted so that his arms are tightly flexed across his chest and his legs unnaturally contorted. Reflex movements in his throat cause him to vomit and dribble. Of all of this, and the presence of members of his family who take turns to visit him, Anthony Bland has no consciousness at all ... The darkness and oblivion ... will never depart.

There was no prospect of any improvement in Bland's condition that could endure for a substantial period. His doctors applied to the court for permission to withdraw his ventilation, antibiotics, and artificial feeding and hydration regime, while continuing otherwise to treat him so as to allow him to die with dignity and minimal pain and suffering. The Official Solicitor (who acts for those under a disability) argued that this would constitute a breach of the doctor's duty to his patient, and a criminal offence.

The House of Lords (the United Kingdom's court of final appeal) regarded the right of self-determination as more important than the right to life. The doctor should respect his patient's rights in that order. This is especially compelling where the patient has, in anticipation of his succumbing to a condition such as PVS, expressed his clear wish not to be given medical care, including artificial feeding, calculated to keep him alive. But, though all five Law Lords agreed that Bland's life should be allowed to end, there is no clear consensus in respect of precisely what the law was or should be. All recognized both the sanctity of life and the autonomy of the patient, but how were these values to be reconciled in the absence of an explicit expression of instructions by Bland? For Lord Goff, the answer lay in protecting the best interests of the patient. But what interests can an insensate patient have? Lord Goff thought they consisted partly in the anguish and stress to others. Lords Keith and Mustill were doubtful, the latter declaring:

> [I]t seems to me to be stretching the concept of personal rights beyond breaking point to say that Anthony Bland has an interest in ending these sources of others' distress. Unlike the conscious patient he does not know what is happening to his body... The distressing truth which must not be shirked is that the proposed conduct is not in the best interests of Anthony Bland, for he has no best interests of any kind.

This approach seems to echo the stance adopted by several courts in the United States and Canada. In the celebrated decision of the United States Supreme Court of *Cruzan*, for instance (involving a

> The law in the Netherlands sets out in fairly lucid terms the conditions that must be satisfied before a doctor is permitted to end a patient's life.
>
> Doctors involved in voluntary euthanasia or suicide must:
>
> a. be convinced that the patient's request was voluntary, well-considered and lasting
> b. be convinced that the patient's suffering was unremitting and unbearable
> c. have informed the patient of the situation and prospects
> d. have reached the conclusion with the patient that there was no reasonable alternative
> e. have consulted at least one other physician
> f. have carried out the procedure in a medically appropriate fashion.
>
> *Section 293(2) of the Dutch Criminal Code*

patient in a PVS whose parents sought to persuade the court that, though she had not expressed this in a 'living will', their daughter would not have wanted to continue living), it was held that the state had an interest in the sanctity, and hence the preservation, of life. Similarly the state's interest in preserving life looms large in the judgments.

In the event, the House of Lords ruled that the withdrawal of Bland's nutrition and hydration did not constitute a criminal offence because any hope of Bland recovering had been abandoned, and, though the termination of his life was not in his best interests, his best interests in being kept alive had also evaporated along with the justification for the non-consensual regime and the duty to maintain it. In the absence of this duty, the withdrawal of nutrition and hydration was not a criminal offence.

Courts around the world cannot circumvent these distressing dilemmas. Their burden would be considerably eased by the existence of a 'living will' in which an individual stipulates something along the lines of the following: 'If, as a result of physical or mental incapacity, I become unable to participate in decisions concerning my medical care and treatment, and subsequently develop any of the medical conditions described below (from which two independent physicians certify I have no reasonable prospect of recovering), I declare that my life should not be sustained by artificial means.'

Doing what comes naturally

Moral questions have, of course, absorbed philosophers since Aristotle. Theories of natural law have sought to resolve the conflict between what 'is' and what 'ought' to be. Its fundamental contention, in simple terms, is that what naturally *is*, *ought* to be. What occurs in nature is good; we should seek to pursue it. Reproduction is natural; therefore we ought to create offspring. As Cicero, the Roman lawyer, put it:

> True law is right reason in agreement with Nature; it is of universal application, unchanging and everlasting.… It is a sin to try to alter this law, nor is it allowable to attempt to repeal any part of it, and it is impossible to abolish it entirely.… [God] is the author of this law, its promulgator, and its enforcing judge.

Contemporary accounts of natural law owe much to the Catholic Church, especially the careful works of the Dominican, St Thomas Aquinas (1225–74), whose principal work *Summa Theologiae* contains the most comprehensive statement of Christian doctrine on the subject. In the 17th century in Europe, the exposition of complete divisions of the law purported to be based on natural law. Hugo de Groot (1583–1645), or Grotius as he is commonly called, is associated with the secularization of natural law. In his influential work *De Jure Belli ac Pacis*, he asserts that even if God did not exist, natural law would have the same content. This was a significant foundation for the emergent discipline of public international law.

The 18th century saw Sir William Blackstone in England proclaiming the significance of natural law in his *Commentaries on the Laws of England*. Blackstone (1723–80) begins his great work by espousing classical natural law doctrine – as if to consecrate English law by this appeal to God-given principles, an attitude that drew the fire of the Utilitarian philosopher and legal and social reformer Jeremy Bentham (1748–1832), who derided natural law as 'a mere work of the fancy'.

Despite his scorn, natural law has been exploited to justify revolutions – especially the American and the French – on the ground that the law infringed individuals' *natural* rights. The American Revolution against British colonial rule was founded on an appeal to the natural rights of all Americans, in the lofty words of the Declaration of Independence of 1776, to 'life, liberty and the pursuit of happiness'. As the Declaration puts it, 'We hold these truths to be self-evident, that all men are created equal, that they are endowed by their Creator with certain unalienable rights.' Equally rousing sentiments were included in the French *Declaration des droits de l'homme et du citoyen* of 26 August 1789, which refers to the 'natural rights' of mankind.

And natural law implicitly underpinned the Nuremberg war trials of Nazi officials which established the principle that certain acts constituted 'crimes against humanity' even if they did not violate particular provisions of the positive law. The judges in these trials did not appeal explicitly to natural law theory, but their judgments exemplify an essential acknowledgement of the idea that the law is not automatically the exclusive criterion of right and wrong.

Our epoch is one of growing public accountability. Or, more precisely, we now seek to prosecute the perpetrators of genocide and other crimes against humanity, and the impunity enjoyed by malevolent government officials, their collaborators, and military commanders is gradually being eroded. The recent establishment of the International Criminal Court (ICC) at The Hague is a remarkable recognition that evil dictators and their henchmen should not be allowed go scot-free. Although the current United States administration has set its face against the court (principally because of fears both that it would undermine US sovereignty over judicial matters relating to American subjects and because its troops might face prosecution), this may well change under a future president. The court's jurisdiction is confined to 'the most serious crimes of concern to the international community as a whole'. This includes crimes against humanity, genocide, war crimes, and crimes of aggression.

9. The trial and execution of Iraqi dictator Saddam Hussein, while it established the accountability of rulers who commit atrocities, attracted criticism on a number of grounds, including the excessive influence of the United States, the frequent replacement of judges, and the attacks on defence lawyers

The prosecution of Slobadon Miloševic, the former president of Yugoslavia, before the International War Crimes Tribunal ended abruptly in 2006 when the defendant died. He was charged with genocide in Bosnia-Herzogovina, crimes against humanity in Croatia, and offences relating to atrocities in Kosovo. The former prime minister of Rwanda was sentenced to life imprisonment for genocide and crimes against humanity. The trial in Iraq of Saddam Hussein resulted in his execution as well as the execution or imprisonment of several of his cronies.

No serious analysis of law and morals can be conducted without reference to the concept of individual rights. Moral claims are regularly transformed into moral rights: individuals assert their rights to a whole range of goods, including life, work, health, education, and housing. Peoples assert their right to self-determination, sovereignty, free trade. In the legal context, rights have acquired significance so profound that they are sometimes regarded as synonymous with law itself. Declarations of political rights are often perceived as the trademark of contemporary democratic statehood. And the inevitable clash between rival rights is among the distinctive features of a liberal society.

On the international front, a panoply of human rights conventions and declarations attest to the strength of rights talk. The United Nations Universal Declaration of Human Rights of 1948, and the International Covenants on Civil and Political Rights, and on Economic, Social and Cultural Rights in 1976, reveal, at least in theory, a dedication by the international community to the universal conception and protection of human rights. It demonstrates a remarkable degree of cross-cultural accord among nations.

Chapter 4
Courts

Judges are the very personification of the law. The judicial function embodies the dispassionate application of evenhandedness, integrity, and the rule of law. Judges resolve disputes, punish offenders, and, where there is no jury, determine guilt. In the more grandiloquent accounts of law and the legal system, judges are its custodians, guardians of its values: sentinels of justice and fair play.

But it is especially the judges' role in criminal trials that excites public interest. The drama of the law court is irresistible to novelists, playwrights, as well as film and television scriptwriters. In the English-speaking world, several come instantly to mind. Dickens' *Bleak House* is a splendid example. Albert Camus' *The Fall*, Kafka's *The Trial*, and the popular portrayal of the judicial process in Harper Lee's *To Kill a Mockingbird*, Scott Turow's *Presumed Innocent*, John Mortimer's *Rumpole of the Bailey* series, and bestseller John Grisham's novels are other striking examples. Shakespeare provides an unforgettable representation of the idea of justice and the forensic process in *The Merchant of Venice*. Courtroom dramas on film abound. Matinée idols are often cast as plucky advocates: Gregory Peck in the film version of *To Kill a Mockingbird*, Paul Newman in *The Verdict*. And courts and lawyers are the stuff of many a successful television series, of which *Ally McBeal*, *The Practice*, and *LA Law* are merely recent instances.

It is easy to see why court proceedings fascinate and entertain. The theatre of a criminal trial is frequently absorbing. The clash of lawyers, the uncertain fate of the accused, the lurid evidence – all excite a voyeuristic curiosity in the presentation. And occasionally the fictional representation of the judicial process is no less spectacular than authentic trials which, particularly in the United States, are often televised live. Where a celebrity is on trial, cameras in court guarantee an enormous audience of viewers – the more gruesome the alleged crime, the better. Few trials, however, achieve this level of vivacity or glamour; they tend to be dreary and tedious.

While a criminal trial may be enlivened by engaging evidence, civil trials normally lack this spice. The court is engaged in the resolution of a dispute. The lawyers who represent the parties seek to persuade the court of the merits of their case. In a common law trial one side cites a previous judgment, arguing that the present case is sufficiently similar to the earlier one that it ought to be followed. The other side seeks to distinguish this precedent by identifying its subtle differences. This is the essence of legal reasoning. Should the losing party appeal, the arguments will be rehearsed before more senior judges.

Judges unquestionably exercise onerous responsibilities:

> It is an awesome thing to go forward before the judge and await the utterances of his decision ... He symbolizes the merger of conceptual justice with organized coercion, the rational human with the mass brute. In him have been remitted the ideals of his culture and the power to compel submission. When a citizen stands in court he feels the immediate impact of that power; it is all assembled and concentrated there on him.

A leading contemporary legal philosopher, Ronald Dworkin, has memorably remarked that 'courts are the capitals of law's empire, and judges are its princes'. Courts do play a central role in every legal system. But what precisely is that role? What of the political function of judges? What of their appointment, election, and accountability? Is the jury system a valuable element in the administration of criminal justice, especially in complex commercial criminal trials? Is the adversarial system of common law countries superior to the inquisitorial system of civil law jurisdictions?

The role of judges is fundamental to the common law; the centrifugal force of the judicial function drives the legal system both in theory and in practice. And though it may be less significant in the codified systems of Continental Europe, the influence of judges cannot be overstated.

The judge is the archetypal legal institution. In his robed and exalted independence, he represents the very apotheosis of justice. The 'social service' that he renders to the community is, in the words of the English judge Lord Devlin, 'the removal of a sense of injustice'. The neutrality that informs his judgments in the settlement of disputes is nothing short of an article of faith in a free and just society. The dispassionate judge is the quintessence of a democratic system of government. And the ostensible delineation between legislation and adjudication is among its most celebrated hallmarks.

Although this attractive and enduring perception of the judicial function is regarded by cynics as a myth, no amount of scepticism can easily dislodge the image of the judge as keeper of the law, protector and repository of justice. Nor is this to deny that judges are, like all of us, tainted by personal predilections and political prejudices. Yet occasionally it is contended that to acknowledge judicial frailty is, in some sense, subversive, 'as if judges', as the

10. A medieval court of law (c. 1450)

illustrious American judge Benjamin Cardozo put it, 'must lose respect and confidence by the reminder that they are subject to human limitations'.

What is the judicial function?

The judicial enterprise lies at the heart of the legal process. In seeking to unravel the mysteries of how judges decide cases, we are engaged in a quest for the meaning of law itself: a theory of what constitutes law is, of necessity, presupposed in the act of judging, as well as any account of it. The orthodox, so-called 'positivist' model perceives law as a system of rules; where there is no applicable rule or there is a degree of ambiguity or uncertainty, the judge has a discretion to fill in the gaps in the law.

This view has been persuasively challenged by Ronald Dworkin, who denies that law consists exclusively of rules. In addition to rules (which 'are applicable in an all-or-nothing fashion'), there are non-rule standards: 'principles' and 'policies', which, unlike rules, have 'the dimension of weight or importance'. A 'principle' is 'a standard that is to be observed, not because it will advance or secure an economic, political, or social situation ...', but because it is a requirement of justice or fairness or some other dimension of morality'. A 'policy', on the other hand, is 'that kind of standard that sets out a goal to be reached, generally an improvement in some economic, political, or social feature of the community'. When the judge can find no immediately applicable rule, or where no settled rule dictates a decision, the judge is called upon to weigh competing principles, which are no less part of the law for their not being rules. In such 'hard cases', since a judge is not expected to resort to his personal preference in arriving at a decision, he has, contrary to the positivist view, no real discretion. There is always one right answer, and it is the judge's task to find it (in 'hard cases') by weighing competing principles and determining the rights of the parties in the case before him.

This model of adjudication has an obvious appeal to democratic theory: judges do not legislate; they merely enforce those rights that have in the main already been enacted by a representative legislature. Indeed, Dworkin's thesis springs from a concern to 'define and defend a liberal theory of law' and, in contradistinction to the positivists, to 'take rights seriously'. It is principally an argument from democracy; Dworkin's concern to eliminate strong judicial discretion is premised on the offensiveness of judges, who are generally unelected officials unanswerable to the electorate, wielding legislative or quasi-legislative power.

Are courts the best forum for resolving disputes? Can judges be genuinely impartial or objective? What is the purpose of a criminal trial? Are certain courts – such as the United States Supreme Court – too political? Should judges be elected? Is the jury system effective and fair? This chapter will attempt to answer some of these questions.

What is a court?

The ubiquity of conflict among humans necessitates some forum in which they might be amicably resolved. Courts are a prerequisite of all legal systems. They have power, authority – or what lawyers called 'jurisdiction' – over specified criminal, civil, and other matters. This entails that their decisions (which are ultimately supported by force) are accepted as authoritative by the parties, who would be unlikely to do so if they did not trust in the independence and impartiality of the professional judges on the bench.

Courts err. Judges are not exempt from human frailty, and there is thus a need for their mistakes to be rectified. The obvious injustice of a wrongly convicted defendant is assuaged by granting him the right of appeal. Equally, the losing party in a civil case may have legitimate legal grounds upon which to argue that the trial court was mistaken in its interpretation of the law. Appealing to a higher court requires a hierarchy that distinguishes between courts 'of first instance' and appellate courts. Some trial courts operate with a judge and a jury: juries are responsible for making findings of fact under the direction of the judge, who decides the law. This combination constitutes the judgment of the court. In other trial courts, both fact and law are decided by the judge.

Appellate courts in common law jurisdictions review the decisions of trial courts or of lower appellate courts. Their task is generally restricted to considering questions of law: did the trial court, for example, apply and interpret the law correctly? Normally they do not hear evidence of factual issues, though should new evidence have emerged, an appeal court may evaluate it in order to determine whether the case should be remitted to a court of first instance to be retried.

Courts everywhere naturally follow procedures which, in some countries, have grown bulky and Byzantine. In criminal trials, these procedures are broadly differentiated on the basis of the role of the judge. The common law adopts an 'adversarial' system, while civil law countries adopt an 'inquisitorial' (or 'accusatorial') system. While this distinction is frequently exaggerated, the two approaches do differ in a fairly fundamental way. The common law judge acts as a disinterested umpire who rarely descends into the dust of the fray. Civil law judges, on the other hand, play a more active role in the trial.

The Continental *juge d'instruction* is directly involved in the decision whether to prosecute. The office originated in France, and exists in a number of other European countries, including Spain, Greece, Switzerland, the Netherlands, Belgium, and Portugal. He is often portrayed as a cross between a prosecutor and a judge, but this is not strictly accurate, for he does not decide whether to lay a charge; that is a matter for the public prosecutor, from whose office he is completely independent. His principal

11. A senior French judge and legal official in their finery

duty is, as the title implies, to investigate the evidence both for and against the suspect, whom he has the power to interrogate. He will also question victims and witnesses. He may visit the crime scene and attend any post-mortem. In the course of his investigation, he may authorize detention, grant bail, and order searches and seizures of evidence.

It is important to note that his job is not to determine the merits of the case, but to examine the evidence in order to decide whether the suspect should be charged. If he rules in the affirmative, the case is transmitted to a trial court with which he has no connection, and which is not bound to follow his decision. His function is thus not wholly unlike common law committal proceedings or the American grand jury, both of which are designed to screen the evidence to establish whether it crosses the threshold of chargeability. Though supervised by a judge, a grand jury is presided over by a prosecutor. It has the power to subpoena witnesses in pursuit of evidence against the suspect.

Both major systems have their virtues and shortcomings. It is generally asserted – especially by common lawyers – that the common law attaches greater significance and value to the presumption of innocence by placing a heavier burden on the prosecution to prove its case 'beyond reasonable doubt'. This is doubtful. A defendant in a French court is afforded essentially the same rights and protections as one in Florida. All democratic states recognize the presumption of innocence; indeed, it is a requirement of Article 6 of the European Convention on Human Rights which applies to the 46 Council of Europe member states.

Criticism of the adversarial system is not confined to civil lawyers. The occasionally grotesque conduct of criminal trials, especially in America, is an embarrassment to common lawyers. The process sometimes descends into burlesque in which lawyers abuse the adversarial process and appear to lose sight of the purpose of the institution. This is particularly evident in high-profile, televised

12. The acquittal on murder charges of former American football star O. J. Simpson prompted misgivings about the reliability of the jury system, especially when, in the view of many, DNA evidence established unequivocally the defendant's guilt

celebrity trials with overpaid lawyers histrionically playing to the cameras and the jury. Many civil lawyers are also astonished by the way in which the common law criminal justice system appears to benefit affluent defendants who are able to afford large legal teams. The trials of O. J. Simpson and Michael Jackson are only the most conspicuous recent examples.

Common law prosecutions are generally pursued by way of a charge or indictment against the defendant in the name of the government, the state, or, in Britain, the Crown. This normally follows a preliminary hearing of some kind to determine whether the prosecution evidence is adequate. To discharge its burden of proof, the prosecution will call witnesses and present its evidence against the defendant. The defence may then argue that there is 'no case to answer'. If this fails (as it usually does), witnesses and evidence are presented by the defence. Witnesses are cross-examined by the opposing counsel, but the defendant himself has the 'right of silence': he need say nothing in his defence, but should he decide to give evidence, he is required to submit to cross-examination. In the United States this right is protected by the Fifth Amendment to the Constitution. Both sides then present their closing arguments. Where there is a jury, the judge gives them their instructions. Its members then deliberate in private. Some jurisdictions require the jury to return a unanimous verdict, in others a majority suffices.

Sentence

If convicted, the defendant is sentenced. This normally occurs after the court is apprized of his previous criminal record, if he has one, as well as other information about his character. Where he faces the prospect of a custodial sentence, reports may be submitted to the court concerning the defendant's background: his education, family, employment history, and so on. Psychological or medical reports may also be presented, along with evidence, including witnesses to testify to his unimpeachable integrity. This may be followed by a moving plea in mitigation of sentence in which his lawyer attempts to convince the court that the accused is a victim of the cruel vicissitudes and privations of life: poverty, manipulation by others, poor parenting, and other equally powerful forces that were beyond his control and are where the true responsibility for his crime lies.

Every jurisdiction will, of course, have a different range of sentences available to a trial court. These may include imprisonment, a fine, a probation order, a community service order, or a suspended sentence of imprisonment (the term of imprisonment is suspended for, say, two years; if he commits an offence during this period, it may trigger the original sentence).

It is always open to the convicted defendant to appeal to a higher court, which does not hear the case again, but peruses the record of the proceedings in search of any mistakes that could justify a retrial. In certain circumstances, the prosecution may appeal a sentence that it considers too lenient.

Civil trials

The disparity between the common and civil law approaches is less marked in civil trials. French law, however, has come close to eliminating civil trials: the extensive pre-trial preparation undertaken by the *juge de la mise en état* results in the pleadings and evidence being reduced to writing. The lawyers merely present brief summaries of what the court already has before it. Moreover, the standard of proof in French civil trials is no lower in civil cases than it is in criminal trials.

In civil law countries 'ordinary' judges preside over 'ordinary' courts. Their jurisdiction, broadly speaking, involves the application of the civil, commercial, and penal codes, and the legislation that complements the codes. In France, the highest court in the ordinary court structure is the *Cour de Cassation* (Supreme Court of Cassation) which comprises some 100 judges who sit in six rotating specialized panels (five civil and one criminal) and, in certain circumstances, in combined panels or plenary session. It has discretion to review only questions of statutory interpretation. Germany has a number of independent judicial systems, each with its own supreme court. Most civilian systems also incorporate a group of administrative courts with separate jurisdiction.

The adversarial system is adopted also in common law civil trials. Instead of the government or Crown proceeding against the defendant, an aggrieved plaintiff sues the defendant, usually for damages, i.e. monetary compensation (for a tort, breach of contract, or other civil wrong). Both sides are free to call witnesses, and the rules of evidence are broadly the same as in criminal trials. An important difference, however, is that whereas, as we saw, the burden of proof in a criminal trial is 'beyond reasonable doubt', the plaintiff in a civil case need only prove his case 'on a balance of probabilities'.

Who are the judges?

Common law judges are, with the conspicuous exception of the United States, appointed from the ranks of senior barristers, while European Continental judges are recruited in the style of the civil service. They are generally recruited directly from university through some form of public examination with no requirement of previous professional experience. Successful candidates are appointed at the bottom of the career ladder; professional training occurs within the judiciary, with promotions depending on merit. Public competition is considered the most effective method of maintaining the professional standing and the independence of the judiciary. It checks political partiality and nepotism, but the fear of prejudicing promotion may inhibit a true spirit of independence from the executive branch. There is also the likelihood that since private practice is normally significantly more lucrative than a career on the bench, the more gifted law graduate may be discouraged from entering the service.

The position in the United States is complex. The federal courts are divided into three tiers: the Supreme Court, the Circuit Court of Appeals, and the District Court. Under the US Constitution, the president has the power to nominate and, in conjunction with the Senate, appoint judges of all three courts. He nominates candidates to the Senate after receiving recommendations from the Department of Justice and White House staff. The Department of Justice screens prospective nominees, followed by an investigation of the candidate by the FBI. Views are sought on the nominee's suitability from the American Bar Association.

The White House Counsel's Office also plays a role; it works together with the Department of Justice and members of the Senate, and considers recommendations by members of the House of Representatives, state governors, bar associations, and other bodies. The Senate Judiciary Committee scrutinizes the credentials of candidates. Should it reject a nomination, it is returned to the president to produce another name. Nominations by the Senate Judiciary Committee are considered by the Senate in executive sessions. Non-controversial candidates tend to be unanimously confirmed. Of the 154 nominations to the US Supreme Court between 1789 and 2004, only 34 were not confirmed by the Senate. When a contentious nomination is made, however, a debate ensues. An adverse recommendation by the Senate Judiciary Committee inexorably results in rejection of the candidate by the Senate. A successful nominee is formally appointed by the president.

The protracted nature of the process, including filibustering by senators, as well as the predictable ideological dimension of the system, has attracted considerable criticism. Its detractors contend that it undermines the independence of the judiciary. Defenders of the method claim that the president and Senate exercise a vital and legitimate check on the composition and standing of the federal judiciary. At the non-federal level, judges are elected in 21 American states; this is a rarity, not encountered in any other common or civil law jurisdiction. Although it may appeal to the democrat, it inevitably transforms judges into politicians who, to keep their jobs, must appeal to popular sentiments and prejudices. While it may be true that an elective system is preferable to one of nomination under a corrupt government which appoints compliant judges regardless of their ability, few lawyers support what John Stuart Mill called 'one of the most dangerous errors ever yet committed by democracy'.

Dissatisfaction with the method of judicial appointment, based largely on the unrepresentative nature of appointees (few women or members of racial minorities), has led to the adoption of judicial appointments commissions which seek to bring to the process greater transparency and fairness. The commission is charged with responsibility for selection. They exist in some states of the United States, as well as in Canada, Scotland, South Africa, Israel, Ireland, and in a number of other European countries, including England and Wales, where since 2006 it functions as an independent non-departmental public body. Applicants for judicial office are required to submit a nine-page application form; short-listed candidates are interviewed. They are evaluated according to five criteria: intellectual capacity; personal qualities

13. In most common law jurisdictions, female judges are a rarity. In Britain, for example, the first woman was appointed to the House of Lords, the country's highest court, only in 2005. Women judges sit on the highest courts of South Africa, Canada, the United States, and New Zealand. The Supreme Court of Canada (pictured here) had its first female judge in 1982, and three of its nine judges are now women, including the Chief Justice

(integrity, independence, judgement, decisiveness, objectivity, ability, willingness to learn); ability to understand and deal fairly; authority and communication skills; and efficiency.

The politics of the judiciary

Though the US Constitution nowhere explicitly confers on the Supreme Court the power of judicial review, it has, since the seminal case of *Marbury v Madison* in 1803, asserted the right to strike down laws that it regards as in conflict with the provisions of the Constitution. This, the most muscular form of judicial review, entails a court of appointed judges (albeit with Senate approval) exercising control over democratically enacted laws. In doing so, the Court has effected major social and political transformations by declaring as unconstitutional a wide range of legislation by states on matters as diverse as abortion, contraception, racial and sexual discrimination, freedom of religion, speech, and assembly.

The Supreme Court of India has, with broad public support, exhibited a high degree of judicial activism in a number of areas of social, political, and economic life, including marriage, the environment, human rights, agrarian reforms, and the law governing elections. The judges have frequently described the constitution as more than a political document; it is considered an abiding declaration of 'social philosophy'. And this philosophy is steeped in egalitarian values that represent a commitment to reform a society to correspond to the principles of social justice that inspired the framers of the constitution. One striking feature of the court's jurisprudence is the concept of public interest litigation whereby the poor obtain access to the courts. The Court has held that legal redress for the deprived should not be encumbered by the restrictions of the adversarial system. Similarly, it has accorded a liberal interpretation of Article 21 of the Constitution which provides that 'No person shall be deprived of his life or personal liberty except according to procedure established by law.' This has engendered a substantial expansion in substantive individual rights.

Under its post-apartheid constitution, the South African Constitutional Court has the power to interpret the constitution and has handed down far-reaching decisions, including declaring capital punishment to be unlawful and upholding the right to housing, the state's constitutional duty to provide effective remedies against domestic violence, and the right to equality.

Strong judicial review is exemplified by the power of the United States Supreme Court, which may impose its judicial interpretations of the Constitution on other branches of government. Weaker forms of judicial review, on the other hand, permit the legislature and executive to reject such rulings, provided they do so publicly. They are increasingly incorporated in constitutions and legislation (such as Britain's Human Rights Act of 1998, the New Zealand Bill of Rights of 1990, and the Canadian Charter of Rights and Freedoms of 1992).

Critics of judicial review consider objectionable the power of judges over democratically elected legislators. But even if our legislative bodies were genuinely representative, the arguments in support of their being in a stronger position than courts to protect and preserve our rights are, at best, doubtful. Not only are the vicissitudes of government and party politics notoriously susceptible to sectional interest and compromise, to say nothing of corruption, but it is precisely because judges are not 'accountable' in this manner that they are often superior guardians of liberty. Moreover, the judicial temperament, training, experience, and the forensic forum in which rights-based arguments are tested and contested tend, I think, to tip the scales towards their adjudicative, rather than legislative, resolution. Indeed, it is hard to see how the latter would operate in practice. Since the rights in question are, by definition, in dispute, what role could elected parliamentarians play?

Unhappily, one's trust in law-makers is rarely vindicated. Though sometimes contentious, certain fundamental rights are best kept off-limits to legislators, or, at least, beyond the reach of normal party political machinations. Would the civil liberties of African Americans have been recognized sooner without the Supreme Court's historic *Brown* judgment, which held that separate educational facilities for black and white pupils was 'inherently unequal'? Is the South African Constitutional Court more likely to defend human rights than its new, democratic parliament? Have the judgments of the European Court of Human Rights (which, sitting in Strasbourg, considers complaints concerning alleged violations of the European Convention for the Protection of Human Rights and Fundamental Freedoms committed by States Parties) not enhanced civil liberties in, say, Britain? The Court has ruled against the British government on frequent occasions, requiring it to amend its domestic law on a variety of Convention-protected rights, including the right of privacy, the right against the use of corporal punishment, and the rights of mental health patients.

Prejudiced judges?

In recent years, there has been a rising crescendo of complaint over the legitimacy – sometimes even the honesty – of particular judicial conduct. From political conservatives have come charges that judges are overriding the will of the people as expressed in statutes and referenda relating to abortions, gay rights, affirmative action, religion, and other subjects. From political liberals come charges of bias against women, sexual misconduct, harshness toward the interests of minorities, and forced imposition of deeply conservative political views. From both sides ... come charges of overriding the people's views and protecting the professional politicians by striking down term limits. From all venues – even from high-priced corporate lawyers – come charges of frequent tyrannical and arbitrary conduct by trial court judges. Misuse of position and even bribery are known to have sometimes existed. Beyond these matters, my thirty-four years as a law professor or a litigator have persuaded me that there is yet another problem, one that is widespread. It is that judges too often are unwilling to listen to facts or reasons. Rather, they start with predilections heavily favoring one side – predilections which they, of course, deny – and then prove impervious to facts and resulting reasons contrary to their bias ... When judges act on the basis of their prior predilections, ignore facts, and

Trial by jury

In criminal proceedings, the notion of being tried by a jury of 'one's peers' is frequently regarded as an article of faith in the common law system. And certain civil law jurisdictions also employ juries to determine the guilt or innocence of the accused. In France, for example, the judges sit together with the jury, who are also involved in determining the sentence to be imposed.

Jurisdictions differ in respect of the availability of juries. Some restrict them to criminal, and not civil, trials (e.g., France); others prescribe juries for trials of serious crimes (e.g., Canada); while in some countries (e.g., England and Wales) they are used in criminal cases and limited to a few specific civil cases (e.g., defamation).

Most conspicuous are the jury trials in the United States, where juries are available for both civil and criminal proceedings. More than 60% of jury trials are criminal trials, the rest are civil and other trials such as family court proceedings.

"We find the defendant guilty. I mean, why else would he go out and hire the best lawyer in town?"

14. Juries may be influenced by factors other than the evidence

Among the much-vaunted virtues of the jury trial is the extent to which it operates as a curb on the power and influence of the judge. By involving (usually 12) ordinary citizens in the administration of justice, it is argued, the values of the community may be expressed. A group of randomly selected lay persons, it is claimed, is a more democratic arbiter of guilt than a judge, who is perceived, rightly or wrongly, as an agent of the government.

Critics of the jury, on the other hand, normally express unease about the fact that juries, unlike judges, are not required to give reasons for their decision, thereby opening the door to emotion and prejudice, especially when the race of the defendant may be a factor (as, for example, in the infamous Rodney King trial, which had disastrous consequences, see the box below). Doubt is also voiced in respect of the ability of the average juror to comprehend complex scientific or other technical evidence. Complex commercial trials, for example, generate an enormous quantity of highly specialized information. This has led to controversial proposals in Britain and elsewhere to abolish juries in these trials.

Alternative dispute resolution

Dissatisfaction with court-centred resolution of disputes has long been sounded by critics who regard it as, amongst other things, unfair, unduly formal, and exclusive. In the United

Race, Rodney King – and a prejudiced jury?

In 1991, in Los Angeles, several police cars chased Rodney G. King, a robbery parolee who was allegedly speeding. After a police chase during which he jumped a number of red lights, King was eventually forced to stop. Though the two passengers in the car complied with police requests to step out of the car and were subdued with negligible resistance, King apparently refused to comply with police instructions, and was physically assisted in doing so. He was struck up to 56 times by officers wielding metal batons, kicked at least six times, and shot with a Taser electronic stun gun. The beating was administered by three Los Angeles police officers, allegedly on the orders of a police sergeant. Twenty-three other law enforcement officers were also present and observed the assault, but apparently made no effort to stop it. A number of bystanders also witnessed the beating, one of whom videotaped the incident. King suffered extensive injuries, including skull fractures and nerve damage to part of his face.

The jury (consisting of ten whites, a Hispanic, and an Asian) acquitted the defendants. Within hours of the jury's verdict, Los Angeles erupted in riots. When it was over, 54 people were dead, over 7,000 individuals had been arrested, and hundreds of millions of dollars' worth of property had been destroyed.

Though some of the officers were subsequently convicted by a federal court on charges of violating King's constitutional rights, and imprisoned, none of the prosecutions specifically alleged racial motivation. In fact, only at the federal trial did King, giving evidence for the first time, testify that he had been racially abused by the police officers, though he subsequently conceded that he was uncertain whether this was in fact the case.

States, a movement championed alternative dispute resolution (ADR) 'under an umbrella of humanism, communitarianism, and social welfare concerns ... objected to the depersonalization, objectification, and distance they associated with courtroom formality and its dependency on legal professionals'. They advocated more user-friendly, less adversarial procedures. This resulted in legislation facilitating greater use of non-judicial arbitration, especially for the resolution of commercial disputes with an international dimension.

The parties submit their dispute to one or more arbitrators by whose decision (called an 'award') they agree to be bound. Among the perceived advantages of ADR are its speed, lower cost,

Litigation: feisty Americans v sociable English

Although the United States *seems* more like England than like any other European country, the American national character is virtually the opposite of the English. Deference, fatalism, self-restraint, and non-aggressiveness are just about the last characteristics that one would ascribe to Americans. Litigation is a kind of fighting, and Americans are fighters; the modern English, outside of the soccer stadium, are not ... National character may be effect rather than cause, and the character of the legal system may be merely another effect of the same cause, or, more realistically, the same complex of causes. The high degree of physical and social mobility in the United States, the immigrant origins of its population, its racial and ethnic heterogeneity, and the wealth and leisure of its population may be responsible for the feisty and individualistic character of the people and *independently* for a heavy demand for judicial processes of dispute resolution. A more static, uniform, close-knit society may simply have fewer disputes – because people understand each other better, or because the greater likelihood of continued relations or future encounters with each other puts a premium on avoiding conflict – or better informal methods of resolving disputes ...

Richard A. Posner, *Law and Legal Theory in England and America* (Clarendon Press, 1996), pp. 109–10

flexibility, and the provision of specialist arbitrators in disputes of a highly technical nature. But delays are not infrequent, and the cost may be enhanced by the requirement that the parties pay for the arbitrators. In some jurisdictions enforcement of arbitral awards is problematic.

Chapter 5
Lawyers

Lawyers are an indispensable – if unloved – feature of every developed legal system. They are vilified, mocked, and disparaged. The humour of a multitude of lawyer jokes springs from their assault on lawyers' venality, dishonesty, and insensitivity. One jibe asks, 'How can you tell when a lawyer is lying?' The answer: 'His lips are moving'. Another sardonically laments, 'Isn't it a shame how 99 per cent of lawyers give the whole profession a bad name?' Mark Twain is reputed to have quipped, 'It is interesting to note that criminals have multiplied of late, and lawyers have also; but I repeat myself.'

It seems futile to attempt to explain this antipathy which rests on a combination of legitimate discontent with and misunderstanding of the legal profession in most countries. It is certainly true that, along with estate agents, lawyers attract little affection. An independent bar is, however, a vital component of the rule of law; without accessible lawyers to provide citizens with competent representation, the ideals of the legal system ring hollow. And this is acknowledged in most jurisdictions by the provision of legal aid in criminal cases. So, for example, legal aid is a right recognized by Article 6 of the European Convention on Human Rights. It requires that defendants be provided with counsel and, if they are unable to afford their own lawyer, one is made available without charge.

15. Atticus Finch: the lawyer-as-hero as depicted by Gregory Peck in the film of the novel _To Kill a Mockingbird_. Finch unsuccessfully defends a black defendant charged with raping a white woman. A number of American attorneys have claimed that the character inspired them to enter the profession

Hollywood's heroic depiction of the lawyer – replicated in endless television series – vigorously, eloquently pursuing the cause of justice for their client, is a far cry from the reality of real lawyers' lives. Advocacy in court represents a small, though important, part of the profession's work. Most lawyers, however, are preoccupied daily with drafting (contracts, trusts, wills, and other documents), advising clients, conducting negotiations, conveying property, and other rather less glamorous tasks. Yet even if the majority of lawyers never set foot in a court, the essence of lawyering is the battle waged on behalf of the client. In this campaign the skills of advocacy – whether in oral or written form – are paramount. Law is often war, and the lawyer is the warrior.

Common lawyers

To many, the English legal profession, adaptations of which exist in common law jurisdictions of the former British

Commonwealth, appears bizarre – grotesquely anachronistic with its wigs, gowns, and stilted forms of address. Though some of these quaint, archaic features have been eradicated in a few common law countries, they have shown a remarkable tenacity, especially in England. Polls of practitioners and public have proved inconclusive. Wigs on the heads of many barristers and judges seem firmly fixed for some time yet.

Big wigs

Sir: Of course the legal wig is an anachronism. But then so is the yarmulke, the mitre, the biretta, the bearskin, the mortarboard and all other forms of ceremonial headdress. I have already been published in the press on the merit of the wig in promoting anonymity and obscuring decrepitude. Its real importance is, however, a heritage issue. For a family lawyer such as myself, it evidences a golden thread of continuity that stretches back beyond the great statute of 1857, beyond Dr Lushington, and into the wonderful realm of 18th-century family law. It is a heritage recognised whether I appear before the Court of Appeal in London, or before the Court of Appeal of the Cayman Islands, or before the Court of Appeal of Hong Kong (which sits, bewigged, under its vivid red symbol containing five stars signifying the sovereignty of communist China). So far as I am aware, no decision has been made to abolish wigs in civil appeals here and I protest against any proposal to do so.

Nicholas Mostyn QC,
Temple, London EC4. Letters, *The Spectator*, 23 June 2007

The origins of the common law profession are, of course, steeped in English history – and logic is thus not necessarily among its justifications. It is divided between two principal species of lawyer: barristers and solicitors. Barristers (often called 'counsel') constitute a small minority of the legal profession (roughly 10% in most jurisdictions) and, rightly or wrongly, are regarded – especially by themselves – as the superior branch of the profession. Recent years have witnessed a number of fairly sweeping changes, many of which have diminished the privileges of barristers (or 'the Bar'). These reforms have largely been animated by political unease concerning the soaring costs of legal services as a result of the restrictive practices of the Bar.

Barristers have minimal direct contact with their 'lay clients'. They are 'briefed' by solicitors, and it is normally a requirement that during meetings (or 'conferences') with clients the solicitor must be present. An exception is, however, made for certain professions, including accountants and surveyors, who may confer with a barrister without the presence of a solicitor. In most cases, however, dealings must be carried out through the solicitor who is responsible for paying the barrister's fees.

English barristers are 'called' to the Bar by one of the four Inns of Court, ancient institutions that since the 16th century have governed entry to this branch of the profession. Unlike the overwhelming majority of solicitors, barristers have full rights of audience, allowing them to appear before any court. Generally, solicitors have rights of audience only before the lower courts, though in recent years the position has changed and some solicitors, certified as 'solicitor advocates', may represent their clients as advocates in the higher courts. The traditional separation is gradually breaking down. Nevertheless, two major distinctions between the two categories of lawyer remain. First, barristers are invariably instructed by solicitors, rather than directly by the client, whereas clients go directly to solicitors. Second, unlike solicitors, barristers operate as sole practitioners, and are prohibited from forming partnerships. Instead, barristers generally form sets of chambers in which resources and expenses are shared. But it is now possible for barristers to be employed by firms of solicitors, companies, or other institutions as in-house lawyers.

16. Though their attire is often derided as eccentric and anachronistic, barristers in several common law jurisdictions adhere to the wigs and gowns that they have worn for centuries. The tenacity of this tradition is illustrated here by a Hong Kong senior counsel who has 'taken silk' and dons the ceremonial long-bottomed wig and silk gown

Other transformations have occurred. For example, barristers are now permitted to advertise their services and their fees – a hitherto unthinkable commercial contamination. Nor are they limited to practising from a set of chambers; after three years' call, they may work from home.

The split profession has been attacked from a number of quarters. Why, it is not unreasonably asked, should a client effectively pay for two lawyers when, as in the United States, for instance, one will do? The case for fusing the two branches (as has occurred, for instance, in Canada, with the exception of Quebec) has been met by a number of responses. In particular, it is argued by defenders of the status quo that an independent barrister offers a detached, expert evaluation of the client's case. Also, solicitors, especially those from small firms, who often lack a high degree of specialization, may draw on the expertise of a wide range of barristerial skills. This enables them to compete with larger firms who boast numerous specialists.

A fused profession operates in a number of common law jurisdictions. The United States draws no distinction; all are attorneys. Anyone who passes the state bar examination may appear in the courts of that state. Some state appeal courts require attorneys to have a certificate of admission to plead and practise in that court. To appear before a federal court, an attorney requires specific admission to that court's bar. Fusion exists also in the states of South Australia and Western Australia, as well as in New Zealand.

A fundamental tenet of counsel's duty in some common law countries (but not, surprisingly, in the United States) is the so-called 'cab-rank rule' under which 'no counsel is entitled to refuse to act in a sphere in which he practises, and on being tendered a proper fee, for any person however unpopular or offensive he or his opinions may be'. Like a taxi driver who is

> ### Rich pickings
>
> We have in the legal profession a prestigious and influential
> group of practitioners, supposedly there to ensure that
> the law's promises of justice for everyone are satisfied, but
> whose most lucrative work continues to be the handling of
> the problems of the rich rather than the trials of the poor ...
> But in the final analysis, the attraction of the legal profession
> of business and 'property' types of work is understandable,
> given the concentration by the legal profession in general on
> the management and protection of property. It is primarily
> the law, therefore, not the lawyers themselves, which
> highlights the problems of the middle- and upper-middle
> classes at the expense of the poor ...
>
> **Phil Harris, *Introduction to Law*,**
> **7th edn (Cambridge University Press, 2007), p. 444**

generally obliged to accept any passenger, a barrister is bound
to accept any brief unless there are circumstances to justify a
refusal, such as that the area of law lies outside of his expertise
or experience, or where his professional commitments prevent
him from devoting sufficient time to the case. In the absence of
such a rule, advocates would be reluctant to appear on behalf of
abhorrent, immoral, or malevolent clients charged, for example,
with heinous crimes such as child molestation. Nevertheless,
in practice, it is not difficult for a barrister to find a reason why
the brief should not be accepted. Apart from the case involving
an area of law beyond his or her capability, the human element
is always present: time is more easily found for a lucrative brief
than one which concerns an intractable or hopeless case. But it
represents a sound statement of professional duty, emphasizing
the role of lawyer as 'hired gun' who acts fearlessly for any client
regardless of the merits of their case.

A striking feature of the training of common lawyers has been the role of some form of apprenticeship (see below). Indeed, it was only towards the end of the 19th century that English universities taught any law at all. And large-scale university legal education in the United States, Canada, Australia, and New Zealand had to await the 20th century, though some universities had established law schools earlier (notably Harvard in 1817).

Civil lawyers

Lawyers in the civil law world differ fundamentally from their common law colleagues. Indeed, the very concept of a legal profession in the major civil law jurisdictions of Europe, Latin America, Japan, and Scandinavia is problematic. In the words of a leading authority on the subject, 'The common law folk concept of "lawyer" has no counterpart in European languages...' Civil law jurisdictions recognize two categories of legal professionals: the jurist and the private practitioner. The former comprises law graduates, while the latter, unlike the position in common law countries, does not represent the nucleus of the legal profession. Instead, 'other subsets of law graduates take precedence – historically, numerically, and ideologically. These include the magistracy (judges and prosecutors)... civil servants, law professors, and lawyers employed in commerce and industry.'

Students in civil law countries typically decide on their future after graduation. And, as mobility within the profession is limited, in many jurisdictions this choice is likely to be conclusive. They may choose to pursue the career of a judge, a public prosecutor, a government lawyer, an advocate, or notary. *Private* practice is therefore generally divided between advocates and notaries. The former has direct contact with clients, and represents them in court. After graduating from law school, advocates normally serve an apprenticeship with experienced lawyers for a number of years, and then tend to practise as sole practitioners or in small firms.

To become a notary usually requires passing a state examination. Notaries draft legal documents such as wills and contracts, authenticate such documents in legal proceedings, and maintain records on, or provide copies of, authenticated documents. Government lawyers serve either as public prosecutors or as lawyers for government agencies. The public prosecutor performs a twin function. In criminal cases, he prepares the government's case; while in certain civil cases he represents the public interest.

In most civil law jurisdictions, the state plays a considerably more significant role in the training, entry, and employment of lawyers than is the case in the common law world. Unlike the traditional position in common law countries where lawyers qualify by serving an apprenticeship, the state controls the number of jurists it will employ, and the universities mediate entry into private practice.

There are important differences between the two systems in respect of the organization of legal education. Broadly speaking, in most common law jurisdictions (with the conspicuous exception of England – and Hong Kong), law is a postgraduate degree or, as in Australia, New Zealand, and Canada, may be combined with an undergraduate degree in another discipline. In the civil law world, on the other hand, law is an undergraduate course. While the common law curriculum is strongly influenced by the legal profession, the state in civil law jurisdictions exercises a dominant function in this respect. The legal profession in most common law countries administers entry examinations, whereas, given the role of universities as gatekeepers, further examinations are generally redundant, and a law degree suffices.

The function of gatekeeping in common law countries tends to be discharged by apprenticeship with a private practitioner. So, for example, an aspiring barrister must pass the Bar examinations in order to be called to the Bar. In order to practise at the Bar, he is required to serve two six-month pupillages in chambers, attending conferences with solicitors conducted by his pupil master (a more senior barrister), and sitting in court, assisting in preparing cases, drafting opinions, and so on. Pupillage is usually unpaid, although they may now be funded so as to guarantee the pupil's earnings up to a fixed level. During the second six months of pupillage, the barrister may engage in limited practice and be instructed in his own right. With the exception of barristers, lawyers in private practice operate as members of a firm whose size may vary from a single lawyer to mega-firms of hundreds of lawyers.

Regulation of the profession

Bar Associations, Bar Councils, and Law Societies are among the numerous organizations that supervise the admission, licensing, education, and regulation of common lawyers. The civil law prefers the term 'advocates' (which more accurately describes their principal function, and their counterpart organizations are dubbed Chambers, Orders, Faculties, or Colleges of Advocates). Though their designations differ, they generally share a concern to limit the number of lawyers in practice, and defend their monopoly.

In certain jurisdictions (particularly small ones like Belgium and New Zealand), lawyers are admitted and regulated at the national level. Federal states (such as the United States, Canada, Australia, and Germany) inevitably exercise provincial or state regulation. Italian lawyers are admitted at the regional level.

While regulation in some countries is undertaken by the judiciary and, under its aegis, an independent legal profession, lawyers in other jurisdictions, especially in the civil law world, are subject to government control in the shape of the Ministry of Justice.

> ### Lawyers in court
>
> The lawyers have twisted it into such a state of bedevilment that the original merits of the case have long disappeared from the face of the earth. It's about a Will, and the trusts under a Will – or it was, once. It's about nothing but Costs, now. We are always appearing, and disappearing, and swearing, and interrogating, and filing, and cross-filing, and arguing, and sealing, and motioning, and referring, and reporting, and revolving about the Lord Chancellor and all his satellites, and equitably waltzing ourselves off to dusty death, about Costs. That's the great question. All the rest, by some extraordinary means, has melted away.
>
> **Charles Dickens**, *Bleak House*, Chapter VIII

Legal aid

Many societies grant legal aid to persons incapable of paying for a lawyer. The right of access to justice rings hollow without the provision of free legal advice and assistance to the poor, especially in criminal cases. Even in respect of civil litigation, however, elementary norms of fairness would be undermined where an impecunious defendant is sued by an affluent plaintiff or the state. Any semblance of equality before the law is thereby shattered. The cost involved (to both the state and the individual seeking legal aid) generally results in preference being given to assisting those charged with criminal offences, though some jurisdictions supply free legal aid in civil cases. Certain systems of legal aid provide lawyers who are employed exclusively to act for eligible, impoverished clients. Others appoint private practitioners to represent such individuals.

"I think your best bet is to plead guilty and then break out of jail."

17. Lawyers can only do so much for their clients

Gideon's right to representation

Gideon was charged in a Florida state court with having broken and entered a poolroom with intent to commit a misdemeanour. Appearing in court without funds and without a lawyer, he asked the court to appoint counsel for him. The following dialogue took place:

The Court: Mr Gideon, I am sorry, but I cannot appoint Counsel to represent you in this case. Under the laws of the State of Florida, the only time the Court can appoint Counsel to represent a Defendant is when that person is charged with a capital offense. I am sorry, but I will have to deny your request to appoint Counsel to defend you in this case.

Gideon: The United States Supreme Court says I am entitled to be represented by Counsel.

Gideon conducted his own defence, was convicted, and sentenced to five years' imprisonment. He then appealed on the ground that the trial court's refusal to appoint counsel for him denied him rights 'guaranteed by the Constitution and the Bill of Rights by the United States Government'. The State Supreme Court rejected his appeal. From his prison cell, Gideon appealed to the US Supreme Court on the ground that he had been denied counsel and therefore that his rights under the Fourteenth Amendment had been violated without due process of law. He was assigned a prominent lawyer, Abe Fortas (later appointed a Justice of the Supreme Court). The court held that the right to the assistance of counsel was a fundamental right, essential for a fair trial, thus emphasizing the procedural safeguards required for due process of law. The defendant's wealth or educational standing should be irrelevant to the question of legal representation. The case was remanded to the Supreme Court of Florida for 'further action not inconsistent with this decision'. Gideon was retried, this time with legal representation, and was acquitted.

Chapter 6
The future of the law

Law, like war, appears to be an inescapable fact of the human condition. But what is its future? The law is, of course, in a constant state of flux. This is nicely expressed by the illustrious American Supreme Court Justice Benjamin Cardozo:

> Existing rules and principles can give us our present location, our bearings, our latitude and longitude. The inn that shelters us for the night is not the journey's end. The law, like the traveller, must be ready for the morrow. It must have a principle of growth.

In a rapidly changing world, growth and adaptation are more pressing than ever if the law is to respond adequately to the new threats as well as novel challenges it faces. The character of law has unquestionably undergone profound transformations in the last 50 years, yet its future is contentious. Some argue that the law is in its death throes, while others postulate a contrary prognosis that discerns numerous signs of law's enduring strength. Which is it? Curiously, there is some truth in both standpoints.

On the one hand, though reports of the death of law have been exaggerated, there is ample evidence of the infirmity of many advanced legal systems. Symptoms include the privatization of law (settlement of cases, plea-bargaining, ADR, the spectacular rise of regulatory agencies with wide discretionary powers, and the decline of the rule of law in several countries). On the other hand, there has been a revolution in the role of law that suggests it is both resilient and robust. This transformation includes the extension of the law's tentacles into the private domain in pursuit of efficiency, social justice, or other political goals; the globalization of law and its internationalization through the United Nations, regional organizations, and the European Union; and the massive impact of technology on the law.

This chapter attempts to uncover some of the major shifts in contemporary society and the formidable challenges they pose to the law.

Law and change

Various attempts have been made to chart the course of legal development. Legal historians have sought to identify the central features in the evolution of law, and, hence, to situate different societies along this continuum. In the late 19th century, the eminent scholar Sir Henry Maine contended that law and society had previously progressed 'from status to contract'. In other words, in the ancient world individuals were closely bound by status to traditional groups, whereas in modern societies individuals are regarded as autonomous beings, they are free to enter into contracts and form associations with whomever they choose.

But some detect a reversal in this movement, and that in many instances freedom of contract is more apparent than real. For example, what choice does the consumer have when faced with a standard-form contract (or contract of adhesion) for telecommunications, electricity, or other utilities? And where is the employee who, when offered a job and presented with a standard-form contract by his multinational employee, would attempt to renegotiate the terms? It is true that many advanced legal systems seek to improve the bargaining position of the individual through various forms of consumer protection legislation. Yet when a lightweight steps into the ring with a heavyweight, the outcome is rarely in doubt. Has 'status' returned in the shape of consumer or employee?

The growth of legal systems also exercised the minds of social theorists. The ideas of Max Weber have exerted a powerful influence on thinking about law and its development. He developed a 'typology' of law based on the different categories of legal thought. At its heart is the idea of 'rationality'. He distinguishes between 'formal' systems and 'substantive' systems. The core of this distinction is the extent to which a system is 'internally self-sufficient', i.e., the rules and procedures required for decision-making are available within the system. Second, he draws a distinction between 'rational' and 'irrational' systems. This describes the manner in which the legal rules and procedures are applied. The highest stage of rationality is reached when all legal propositions constitute a logically clear, internally consistent system of rules under which every conceivable fact or situation is included.

Weber gives as an example of a formally legal irrational system the phenomenon of trial by ordeal where guilt is determined by an appeal to some supernatural force. An example of substantive legal irrationality is where a judge decides a case on the basis of his personal opinion without any reference to rules. A decision of a judge is substantively rational, according to Weber, when he refers not to rules but moral principles or concepts of justice. Finally, where a judge defers to a body of doctrine consisting of legal rules and principles, the system constitutes one of formal logical legal rationality. It is towards this ideal type that Weber's theory of legal evolution progresses.

In many societies, however, Weber's model of a rational, comprehensive, and coherent legal system is undermined by the rapid rise in administrative control. There has been a colossal expansion in the jurisdiction of administrative agencies. These bodies, normally creatures of statute, are vested with extensive discretionary powers. In some cases, their decisions are explicitly exempted from judicial oversight.

In several European countries, for example, the privatization of formerly nationalized industries (such as utilities and telecommunications) has spawned a host of regulatory agencies with powers to investigate, make rules, and impose penalties. The ordinary courts may be marginalized, and hence the role of law itself becomes distorted. This development represents a threat to the authority and openness of courts. Moreover, the enlargement of discretionary powers emasculates the rule of law's insistence on the observance of clear rules that specify individual rights and duties. Discretionary regulation resembles Weber's notion of substantive legal rationality, while the ideology of the rule of law represents formal legal rationality.

Among the more radical theories of legal development is the Marxist idea that law is ultimately doomed to disappear entirely. This prediction is grounded in the idea of historicism: social evolution is explained in terms of inexorable historical forces. Marx and Engels propounded the theory of 'dialectical materialism' which explains the unfolding of history in terms of the development of a thesis, its opposite (or antithesis) and, out of the ensuing conflict, its resolution in a synthesis. Marx argued that each period of economic development has a corresponding class system. During the period of hand-mill production, for instance, the feudal system of classes existed. When steam-mill production developed, capitalism replaced feudalism. Classes are determined by the means of production, and therefore an individual's class is dependent on his relation to the means of production. Marx's 'historical materialism' is based on the fact that the means of production are materially determined; it is dialectical, in part, because he sees an inevitable conflict between those two hostile classes. A revolution would eventually occur because the bourgeois mode of production based on individual ownership and unplanned competition, stands in opposition to the increasingly non-individualistic, social character of labour production in the factory. The proletariat would, he predicted, seize the means of production and establish a 'dictatorship of the proletariat' which would, in time, be replaced by a classless, communist society in which law would eventually 'wither away'. Since the law is a vehicle of class oppression, it is superfluous in a classless society. This is the spirit of the argument first implied by Marx in his early writings and restated by Lenin. In its more sophisticated version the thesis claims that, following the proletarian revolution, the bourgeois state would be swept aside and replaced by the dictatorship of the proletariat. Society, after reactionary resistance has been defeated, would have no further need for law or state: they would 'wither away'.

But this cheerful prognosis is based on a rather crude equation of law with the coercive suppression of the proletariat. It disregards the fact not only that a considerable body of law serves other functions, but that, even, or especially, a communist society requires laws to plan and regulate the economy. To claim that these measures are not 'law' is to elicit incredulity.

Whatever theory is adopted to explain the manner and form of legal change, it is impossible to deny that the future of law is beset with a host of thorny challenges. Where might the greatest difficulties lie?

Internal challenges

In addition to the problem of bureaucratic regulation and the often unbridled discretion it generates (discussed above), there are a number of intractable questions that need to be confronted by legal systems everywhere. Some are mentioned in Chapter 2. Among the most conspicuous is the so-called 'war on terror'. It requires little perception to realize that in the space of less than a decade many legal systems are faced with a variety of problems that test the values that lie at their heart. How can free societies reconcile a commitment to liberty with the necessity to confront threats to undermine that very foundation? Absolute security is plainly unattainable, but even moderate protection against terror comes at a price. And no airline passenger can be unaware of the cost in respect of the delays and inconvenience that today's security checks inevitably entail. But though crime can never be entirely prevented, modern technology does offer extraordinarily successful tools to deter and apprehend offenders. Closed circuit television (CCTV) cameras, for instance, are able to monitor unlawful activities, such recordings supplying prosecutors with powerful evidence in court against the filmed villain. To what extent should the law tolerate this kind of surveillance? Consider the following example, which may help to demonstrate the difficulty, and the unavoidable 'balancing' between competing rights that is a conspicuous characteristic of modern law.

I like my car. It's nothing special: but its silver body induces in me a pleasing sensation. Or did. A few days ago, as I was about to unlock the door, I noticed a deep scratch that stretched along the side of the car. A key or perhaps a screwdriver had been dragged over its metallic surface. A similar wound had been inflicted on the bonnet. I was furious. Not unlike a character in a movie, I scoured the vicinity in the vain hope of some sign of the vandal, my face suitably arranged in an expression of ferocious indignation. But the miscreant was long gone. The offence had been committed, I presumed, during the night. I was left to my curses. The car was parked in a well-lit area, but this was plainly no deterrent. Why, I instantly lamented, was there no CCTV camera nearby to record the villain's identity? I wanted him caught and punished.

A trivial instance of criminal damage, perhaps, but it would be ingenuous not to think that most people would support measures that might successfully prevent crime and, especially since 11 September 2001, acts of terrorism. Surely, a terrorist, no less than the delinquent who damaged my car, would be thwarted were a

18. CCTV cameras police the streets of many cities

CCTV to record his (or, less likely, her) every move? Law-abiding citizens must feel safer in the knowledge that this surveillance is taking place. And why not? Polls confirm their wide support. Who but the robber, abductor, or bomber has anything to fear from the monitoring of his or her activities in public places? Nor should it stop there. Advances in technology render the tracking of an individual's financial transactions and email communications simple. The introduction of 'smart' ID cards, the use of biometrics, and electronic road pricing represent major developments in methods of surveillance. Only the malevolent could legitimately object to these effective methods of crime control. Would that this comforting view were true.

We cannot afford to pussyfoot with terrorists, but how far should we be willing to trade our freedom for security? In the immediate aftermath of the events of 11 September 2001, politicians, especially in the United States, have understandably sought to enhance the powers of the state to detain suspects for interrogation, intercept communications, and monitor the activities of those who might be engaged in terrorism. The law faces formidable difficulties here. Draconian powers are probably unavoidable during times of war: arbitrary powers of arrest and detention, imprisonment without trial, secret trials, and the like. How long can a free society tolerate these infringements of liberty? What lasting damage may be inflicted on the rule of law and individual rights? Can the law continue to protect citizens or will citizens need protection *from* the law? Are the courts able to act as a bulwark against these attacks on freedom?

A vivid example of a society that attempted a comprehensive assault on 'terrorism' is apartheid South Africa. Heavy-handed laws made substantial legislative inroads into the jurisdiction of the courts in the realm of civil liberties. The removal of the authority of the judiciary to question the exercise of executive power under a wide range of circumstances considerably attenuated the authority of judges. The ever-increasing sphere of unchecked executive discretion in matters of fundamental liberty such as detention, deportation, banning, and censorship reduced the members of the judiciary to impotent spectators of administrative action. This was a grotesque distortion of their calling. Moreover, even where a courageous judge was able to interpret the law in favour of liberty, he was, in practice, likely to have his efforts frustrated by legislation to nullify its effect.

A less egregious engine of change is the internationalization or globalization of law. The world has witnessed an escalation in the influence and importance of international (the United Nations) or regional organizations (such as the European Union). These sources of law diminish the authority of domestic law. Nor has the law been spared the McDonald's effect of powerful multinational corporations influencing the character of banking, investments, consumer markets, and so on. All have a direct impact on the law.

Furthermore, most legal systems face unresolved dilemmas in several of the disciplines discussed in Chapter 2. Some of these problems were touched upon there. They are both substantive and procedural, and include several quandaries concerning the criminal justice system. What is the future of the criminal trial in the face of complex commercial offences, often involving sophisticated know-how? Is the jury trial appropriate in these circumstances, or at all? Is the civil law inquisitorial system preferable to the common law adversarial approach? In many jurisdictions, access to the law is patchy. The poor are not always provided with adequate access to the courts and other institutions of dispute resolution. No less prickly issues beleaguer private law. For example, many legal systems wrestle with the difficult question of compensation for personal injuries, and the effect of insurance on the award of damages.

While the law on its own can never transform, or indeed conserve, the social order and its values, it has the capacity to influence and shape attitudes. Efforts to achieve social justice through law have not been an unqualified success. Statutes outlawing racial discrimination, for example, represent only a modest advance in the cause of equality. While little can be accomplished *without* legal intervention, the limits of law need to be acknowledged. There is a growing tendency to legalize moral and social problems, and even to assume that the values underpinning democratic Western legal systems, and their institutions, can be fruitfully exported or transplanted to less developed countries. This may be a Utopian view. Equally sanguine may be the proposition that economic development necessarily presages respect for human rights, as is frequently contended in the case of China.

Modern governments espouse highly ambitious legislative programmes that frequently verge upon social engineering. To what extent can legislation genuinely improve society, combat discrimination and injustice? Or are courts more appropriate vehicles for social change? Where, as in the United States, a vigorous Supreme Court has the clout to declare laws unconstitutional, the legislature has no choice but to fall in line, as it did following the seminal case of *Brown v Board of Education of Topeka* in 1954. A unanimous court declared the establishment of separate public schools for black and white students 'inherently unequal'. This landmark decision opened the doors (literally) to integration and the birth of the Civil Rights Movement. Though discrimination will always exist, few would deny that the case changed the law – and society – for the better.

Da Vinci's code

The time will come when people such as I will look upon the murder of (other) animals as they now look upon the murder of human beings.

Leonardo da Vinci

19. Whatever legal status we accord animals, a major obstacle in the path of genuine protection of their welfare is the inadequate enforcement of the law

Without effective enforcement, laws cannot fulfil their noble aspirations. Legislation prohibiting animal cruelty is a case in point. Vivisection, battery farming, the fur trade, hunting, trapping, circuses, zoos, and rodeos are merely some of the practices, apart from the direct intentional infliction of pain on an animal, that cause misery and suffering to millions of creatures around the world every day. Anti-cruelty statutes have been enacted in many jurisdictions, yet in the absence of rigorous enforcement, these laws constitute mostly empty promises. And enforcement is a major hurdle: detection is largely dependent on inspectors who lack the power of arrest, prosecutors who rarely regard animal cruelty cases as a high priority, and judges who seldom impose adequate punishment, not that the statutory penalty is itself sufficiently stringent.

In an increasingly anxious world, there is an understandable tendency to look to the law to resolve the manifold threats to our future. In recent years, the dangers of pollution, depletion of the

The law and the suffering of animals

The day may come, when the rest of the animal creation may acquire those rights which never could have been withholden from them but by the hand of tyranny. The French have already discovered that the blackness of skin is no reason why a human being should be abandoned without redress to the caprice of a tormentor. It may come one day to be recognized, that the number of legs, the villosity of the skin, or the termination of the os sacrum, are reasons equally insufficient for abandoning a sensitive being to the same fate. What else is it that should trace the insuperable line? Is it the faculty of reason, or perhaps, the faculty for discourse? ... [T]he question is not, Can they reason? nor, Can they talk? but, Can they suffer? Why should the law refuse its protection to any sensitive being? ... The time will come when humanity will extend its mantle over everything which breathes ...

Jeremy Bentham,
Introduction to the Principles of Morals and Legislation

ozone layer, global warming, and other threats to the survival of many species of animal, marine, bird, and plant life have assumed a higher profile. A growing number of states have introduced legislation to attempt to limit or control the destruction of the planet. The law, however, often proves to be a rather blunt instrument. For example, in the case of the criminal liability of a company for pollution, a conviction depends on proof that those who control the company had the requisite knowledge or intention. This is notoriously difficult to prove. And even where these acts are strict liability offences, the fines imposed by courts have a limited deterrent effect. It may be that the numerous international treaties, conventions, and declarations on almost every aspect of environmental protection are likely to be more effective, though, as with the law, the predictable stumbling block is effective enforcement.

Technological challenges

There is nothing new about the law's struggle to keep abreast with technology. Yet the last 20 years have witnessed an unprecedented transformation of the contest. Digital disquiet easily spawns alarm and anxiety. The emergence of information technology, to select only one obvious instance, poses enormous challenges to the law. Attempts legally to control the Internet, its operation or content, have been notoriously unsuccessful. Indeed, its very anarchy and resistance to regulation is, in the minds of many, its strength and attraction. But is cyberspace beyond regulation? The distinguished legal academic Lawrence Lessig has persuasively argued that it is susceptible to control, not necessarily by law, but through its essential make-up, its 'code': software and hardware that constitute cyberspace. That code, he suggests, can either produce a place where freedom prevails or one of oppressive control. Indeed, commercial considerations increasingly render cyberspace decidedly amenable to regulation; it has become a place in which conduct is more strongly controlled than in real space. In the end, he maintains, it is a matter for us to determine; the choice is one of architecture: what sort of code should govern cyberspace, and who will control it? And in this respect, the central legal issue is code. We need to choose the values and principles which should animate that code.

Information is no longer merely power. It is big business. In recent years, the fastest growing component of international trade is the service sector. It accounts for more than one-third of world trade – and continues to expand. It is a commonplace to identify, as a central feature of modern industrialized societies, their dependence on the storage of information. The use of computers facilitates, of course, considerably greater efficiency and velocity in the collection, storage, retrieval, and transfer of information. The everyday functions of the state as well as private bodies require a continual supply of data about individuals in order to administer effectively the numerous services that are integral to contemporary life and the expectations of citizens. Thus, to mention only the most conspicuous examples, the provision of health care, social security, and the prevention and detection of crime by the law enforcement authorities assume the accessibility of a vast quantity of such data, and, hence, a willingness of the public to furnish them. Equally in the private sector, the provision of credit, insurance, and employment generate an almost insatiable hunger for information.

Big Brother?

The future is unlikely to witness an escalation of our privacy. Can the law curb the apparently relentless slide towards an Orwellian nightmare? 'Low-tech' collection of transactional data in both the public and private sector has become commonplace. In addition to the routine surveillance by CCTV in public places, the monitoring of mobile telephones, the workplace, vehicles, electronic communications, and online activity are increasingly taken for granted in most advanced societies. The escalating use of surveillance in the workplace, for example, is changing not only the character of that environment, but also the very nature of what we do and how we do it. The knowledge that our activities are, or even may be, monitored, undermines our psychological and emotional autonomy. Indeed, the slide towards electronic supervision may fundamentally alter our relationships and our identity. In such a world, employees are arguably less likely to execute their duties effectively. If that occurs, the snooping employer will, in the end, secure the precise opposite of what he hopes to achieve.

The privacy prognosis is not encouraging; the future promises more sophisticated and alarming intrusions into our private lives, including the greater use of biometrics, and sense-enhanced searches such as satellite monitoring, penetrating walls and clothing, and 'smart dust' devices (minuscule wireless micro-electromechanical sensors (MEMS) that can detect

20. Sinn Fein President, Gerry Adams, displays the sophisticated listening equipment and digital tracking device discovered in a car used by the party

everything from light to vibrations). These so-called 'motes' – as tiny as a grain of sand – would collect data that could be sent via two-way band radio between motes up to 1,000 feet away.

As cyberspace becomes an increasingly perilous domain, we learn daily of new, alarming assaults on its citizens. This slide towards pervasive surveillance coincides with the mounting fears, expressed well before 11 September, about the disturbing capacity of the new technology to undermine our liberty. Reports of the fragility of privacy have, of course, been sounded for at least a century. But in the last decade they have assumed a more urgent form. And here lies a paradox. On the one hand, recent advances in the power of computers have been decried as the nemesis of whatever vestiges of our privacy still survive. On the other, the Internet is acclaimed as a Utopia. When clichés contend, it is imprudent to expect sensible resolutions of the problems they embody, but between these two exaggerated claims, something resembling the truth probably resides. In respect of the future of privacy, at least, there can be little doubt that the legal questions are changing before our eyes. And if, in the flat-footed domain of atoms, we have achieved only limited success in protecting individuals against the depredations of surveillance, how much better the prospects in our brave new binary world?

When our security is under siege, so – inevitably – is our liberty. A world in which our every movement is observed erodes the very freedom this snooping is often calculated to protect. Naturally, we need to ensure that the social costs of the means employed to enhance security do not outweigh the benefits. Thus, one unsurprising consequence of the installation of CCTV in car parks, shopping malls, airports, and other public places is the displacement of crime; offenders simply go somewhere else. And, apart from the doors this intrusion opens to totalitarianism, a surveillance society can easily generate a climate of mistrust and suspicion, a reduction in the respect for law and those who enforce it, and an intensification of prosecution of offences that are susceptible to easy detection and proof.

Though data protection legislation has been enacted in more than 30 jurisdictions, its scope is limited. At its core is the simple proposition that data relating to an identifiable individual should not be collected in the absence of a genuine purpose and the consent of the individual concerned. At a slightly higher level of abstraction, it encapsulates the principle of what the German Constitutional Court has called 'informational self-determination' – a postulate that expresses a fundamental democratic ideal. But the enactment of data protection legislation is driven only partly by altruism. The new information technology disintegrates national borders; international traffic in personal data is a routine feature of commercial life. The protection afforded to personal data in Country A is, in a digital world, rendered nugatory when it is retrieved on a computer in Country B in which there are no controls over its use. Hence, states with data protection laws frequently proscribe the transfer of data to countries that lack them. Indeed, the European Union has in one of its several directives explicitly sought to annihilate these 'data havens'. Without data protection legislation, countries risk being shut out of the rapidly expanding information business.

At the heart of these laws are two central canons of fair information practice that speak for themselves: the 'use limitation' and 'purpose specification' principles. They require rejuvenation where they already exist, and urgent adoption where they do not (most conspicuously, and indefensibly, in the United States). They may, moreover, be able to provide complementary safeguards for individual privacy in cyberspace.

The future of the right to privacy depends in large part on the ability of the law to formulate an adequately clear definition of the concept itself. This is not only a consequence of the inherent vagueness of the notion of privacy, but also because the 'right of

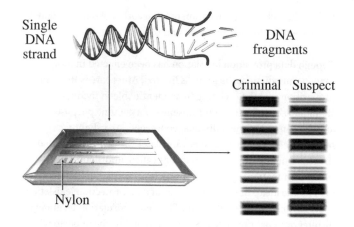

Single DNA strand

DNA fragments

Criminal   Suspect

Nylon

21. The use of DNA evidence has become a routine feature of criminal investigation in many countries

privacy' has conspicuously failed to provide adequate support to the private realm when it is intruded upon by competing rights and interests, especially freedom of expression. In our burgeoning information age, the vulnerability of privacy is likely to intensify unless this central democratic value is translated into simple language that is capable of effective regulation.

Other developments have comprehensively altered fundamental features of the legal landscape. The law has been profoundly affected and challenged by numerous other advances in technology. Computer fraud, identity theft, and other 'cybercrimes', and the pirating of digital music, are touched on below. Developments in biotechnology such as cloning, stem cell research, and genetic engineering provoke thorny ethical questions and confront traditional legal concepts. Proposals to introduce identity cards and biometrics have attracted strong objections in several jurisdictions. The nature of criminal trials has been transformed by the use of both DNA and CCTV evidence.

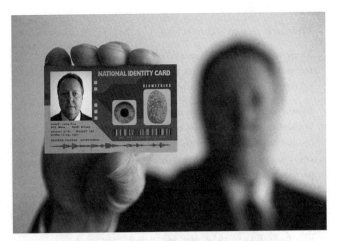

22. **ID cards of various kinds are widespread throughout the world, though fairly rare in common law jurisdictions. The rise in international terrorism has fuelled the demand for their introduction in several countries. But their capacity to merge personal information from numerous sources poses threats to individual privacy**

Big Brother already appears to be alive and well in several countries. Britain, for example, boasts more than 4 million CCTV cameras in public places: roughly one for every 14 inhabitants. It also possesses the world's largest DNA database, comprising some 3.6 million DNA samples. The temptation to install CCTV cameras by both the public and private sector is not easy to resist. Data protection law ostensibly controls its use, but such regulation has not proved especially effective. A radical solution, adopted in Denmark, is to prohibit their use, subject to certain exceptions such as petrol stations. The law in Sweden, France, and Holland is more stringent than in the United Kingdom. They adopt a licensing system, and the law requires that warning signs be placed on the periphery of the zone monitored. German law has a similar requirement.

The dark side of biometrics

Biometrics is one of the most serious among the many technologies of surveillance that are threatening the freedom of individuals and of societies.

In one possible future, biometrics will fall into ill-repute in relatively free countries. But in authoritarian countries, biometrics will be successfully imposed on the population, resulting in freedoms being reduced even further. Biometrics providers will flourish by selling their technology to repressive governments, and achieve footholds in relatively free countries by looking for soft targets, starting in some cases with animals, and in others with captive populations like the frail aged, prisoners, employees, insurance consumers, and welfare recipients. All relatively free countries will become more repressive. Public confidence in corporations and government agencies will spiral much lower. This scenario leads away from freedoms, and towards subjugation of the individual to powerful organizations.

The other alternative is that societies appreciate the seriousness of the threats, and impose substantial constraints on technologies and their use. This demands commitment by the public, and courage by elected representatives, who must withstand pressure from large corporations, and from the national security and law enforcement apparatus that invokes such bogeymen as terrorism, illegal immigration, and domestic law and order as justifications for the implementation of repressive technologies. This scenario embodies scope for achieving balance among the needs of individuals and society as a whole.

Roger Clarke, 'Biometrics and Privacy'
http://www.anu.edu.au/people/Roger.Clarke/DV/Biometrics.html

In order to counter the threat of terrorism, the future will unquestionably witness an increased use of biometrics. Biometrics includes, in particular, a number of measures of human physiography such as fingerprints, aspects of the iris and ear lobes, and DNA. The Australian privacy advocate Roger Clarke provides the following examples of characteristics on which biometric technologies can be based: one's appearance (supported by still images), e.g., descriptions used in passports, such as height, weight, colour of skin, hair, and eyes, visible physical markings, gender, race, facial hair, wearing of glasses; natural physiography, e.g., skull measurements, teeth and skeletal injuries, thumbprint, fingerprint sets, handprints, retinal scans, ear lobe capillary patterns, hand geometry, DNA patterns; bio-dynamics, e.g., the manner in which one's signature is written, statistically analysed voice characteristics, keystroke dynamics, particularly login-ID and password; social behaviour (supported by video-film), e.g., habituated body signals, general voice characteristics, style of speech, visible handicaps; imposed physical characteristics, e.g., dog tags, collars, bracelets and anklets, bar codes and other kinds of brands, embedded micro-chips and transponders. The law will need to respond to this dangerous trend.

New wrongs and rights

Advances in technology are predictably accompanied by new forms of mischief. Today it is 'podslurping' (see below); tomorrow it is another evil facilitated by the digital world we now inhabit. The law is not always the most effective or appropriate instrument to deploy against these novel depredations. Technology itself frequently offers superior solutions. In the case of the Internet, for example, a variety of measures exist to protect personal data online. These include the encryption, economization, and erasure of personal data.

While new-fangled wrongs will continue to emerge, some transgressions are simply digital versions of old ones. Among the more obvious novel threats, there are a number which tease the law's capacity to respond to new offences. These include complex problems arising largely from the ease with which data, software, or music may be copied. The pillars upon which intellectual property law was constructed have been shaken. This incorporates the law of patents (see below) and trademarks, especially in respect of domain names. Defective software gives rise to potential contractual and tortious claims for compensation. The storage of data on mobile telephones and other devices relentlessly tests the law's ability to protect the innocent against the 'theft' of information. New threats emerge almost daily. Employers have been warned of the relative ease with which their workers may appropriate data by 'podslurping', a simple operation that consists in the unauthorized downloading of data from a computer to a small device such as an iPod, MP3 player, or flash drive.

Internet iniquity

Malevolent websites are multiplying by the day. A study by Google in May found 450,000 booby-trapped pages out of a sample of 4.5 million pages. A further 700,000 looked likely to be dangerous. Most of the websites exploit weaknesses in Microsoft's Internet Explorer browser ... increasingly common are sites that steal private details or turn your computer into a 'bot' – one which is remotely controlled by someone else. Bots can be used to harvest email addresses, send spam and conduct attacks on corporate websites. Then there are the 'Denial of Service' (DoS) attacks, which use armies of 'bots' – or 'zombies' – to flood company websites with fake data requests. The words conjure up images from Night of the Living Dead and the reality is the online equivalent of consuming a living person's flesh, as hundreds of thousands of 'zombies' attack a website until they've taken it offline – which can disable it for days and lose the company a fortune. Usually the attacks are accompanied by demands for money. Gambling and porn sites were among the first to get hit: reluctant to seek police help, they paid the ransom – often to accounts in Russia or Eastern Europe ... Of course there are defences against hackers, and you'd be mad not to install anti-virus, anti-spyware and anti-spam software on your personal computer ... [T]he future looks even more terrifying. Simon Church of VeriSign says the online auction sites that criminals use to sell user details are just the beginning. He foresees one of the web's current favourites – 'mashup' sites that put together different databases – being turned to illicit use. 'Imagine if a hacker put together information he'd harvested from a travel company's database with Google Maps. He could provide a tech-savvy burglar with the driving directions of how to get to your empty house the minute you go on holiday.' I don't know about you, but that's enough to make me resort to carrier pigeons and cash.

Edie G. Lush, 'How Cyber-Crime Became
a Multi-Billion-Pound Industry', *The Spectator*, 16 June 2007

Criminals have not been slow to exploit the law's frailties. Cybercrime poses new challenges for criminal justice, criminal law, and law enforcement both nationally and internationally. Innovative online criminals generate major headaches for police, prosecutors, and courts. This new terrain incorporates cybercrimes against the person (such as cyber-stalking and cyber-pornography), and cybercrimes against property (such as hacking, viruses, causing damage to data), cyber-fraud, identity theft, and cyber-terrorism. Cyberspace provides organized crime with more sophisticated and potentially more secure methods for supporting and developing networks for a range of criminal activities, including drug and arms trafficking, money laundering, and smuggling.

Protecting software

Complex legal (and, in the United States, constitutional) issues
surround the question of patenting software. A patent is the
grant of an exclusive right to exploit or develop an invention.
With the introduction of various forms of computer programs
and other types of software, the law will continue to grapple
with challenging, and often perplexing, problems as to whether
there is sufficient novelty in the software to justify patentability.
In general, the law takes the view that computer programs are
not patentable unless they constitute a genuine invention with
industrial application.

There is, on the other hand, a greater readiness to provide
copyright protection to software, web pages, and even email
messages since their owners have, as the name implies, the right
to copy the material and, by extension, the right to prevent others
from doing so. Software piracy has grown into a significant
menace to major software producers such as Microsoft, but the
issue is extremely controversial since, though it is clear that
certain countries (China, Vietnam) engage in the wholesale
copying of software, it is argued that the huge losses (up to 12
billion US dollars) that companies such as Microsoft claim they
suffer is illusory because many of those who purchase pirated
software are unable to afford legitimate versions. Moreover, it is
contended by opponents of copyright for computer programs such
as the Free Software Foundation that '"free software" is a matter
of liberty, not price. To understand the concept, you should think
of "free" as in "free speech," not as in "free beer." Free software is a
matter of the users' freedom to run, copy, distribute, study, change
and improve the software.'

But, as mentioned above, some wrongs have simply undergone a
digital rebirth. For example, the tort of defamation has found a
congenial new habitat in cyberspace. The law in most jurisdictions

protects the reputation of persons through the tort of defamation or its equivalent. It will be recalled that while there are variations within common law jurisdictions, the law generally imposes liability where the defendant intentionally or negligently publishes a false, unprivileged statement of fact that harms the plaintiff's reputation. Civil law systems, instead of recognizing a separate head tort of defamation protect reputation under the wing of rights of the personality. In cyberspace, however, national borders tend to disintegrate, and such distinctions lose much of their importance.

The advent of email, chat rooms, bulletin boards, newsgroups, and blogs provide fertile ground for defamatory statements online. Since the law normally requires publication to only one person other than the victim, an email message or posting on a newsgroup will suffice to found liability. But it is not merely the author of the libel who may be liable.

In an important, if somewhat unclear, decision, a New York court held an Internet service provider, Prodigy, responsible for defamatory statements that appeared on its bulletin boards. The basis of the judgment was that Prodigy was a 'publisher' – principally because it had exercised editorial control over the content of its bulletin boards. In pursuit of this objective, it had posted 'content guidelines' to its users, and it employed a software screening program to screen postings for offensive language. An earlier New York decision had decided that another service provider, CompuServe, was not liable for defamatory statements that appeared on one of its online forums. The judgment was based on the fact that the defendants were merely distributors rather than actual publishers. It was the functional equivalent of a lending library. Under these circumstances, free speech should prevail. An English decision that settled before a full trial was held rejected the ISP's argument that it was merely an innocent purveyor of information.

Tomorrow's courts and lawyers

It is not merely the law but its institutions and practitioners whose future will be profoundly affected by the developments in information technology. It is improbable that judges will be replaced by computers (though this prospect is not without its supporters), but the administration of justice in many advanced societies has already undergone significant changes and will continue to do so. The courts of several jurisdictions already benefit from access to legal materials that previously would have consumed long hours of research. Virtual law libraries with sophisticated search facilities enable judges, lawyers, legal academics, and ordinary members of society to obtain rapid access to statutes, cases, and other sources of law. This will be especially helpful to less affluent countries with limited legal resources. Increasingly, judgments of the courts are posted on the Internet almost immediately after they have been handed down. There are already several excellent online legal databases such as findlaw.com and austlii.com.

The electronic transcription of court proceedings, the management of cases, and standardization of electronic documents will continue to enhance the judicial process, streamlining and reducing notorious delays. The sight of a judge laboriously taking written notes is already disappearing, but voice-recognition technology will obviate the need for note-taking of any kind. Both evidence and legal sources can effortlessly be retrieved electronically. A more radical development might be the establishment of virtual courts in which the parties conduct proceedings without the need for corporeal proximity, thereby decreasing cost and delay.

Many of these advances (and there will be others) are likely to generate significant advantages for the ordinary individual seeking access to justice. Once legal information and services become more widely available, it ought to follow that the grandiose ambitions of the law and legal system will be more effectively accomplished. The role of lawyers and the administration of justice will, in the words of Richard Susskind:

> no longer be dominated by print and paper in tomorrow's legal paradigm. Instead, legal systems of the information society will evolve rapidly under the considerable influence of ever more powerful information technologies. We will no longer suffer from the excessive quantity and complexity of legal material. There will be mechanisms in place to give everyone fair warning of the existence of new law and changes in old. Legal risks will be managed in advance of problems occurring and so dispute pre-emption rather than dispute resolution will be the order of the day. Our law will thus become far more fully integrated with our domestic, social and business lives.

Who would not welcome this sanguine prophecy?

The death of copyright?

The anarchist revolution in music is different from the one in software *tout court*, but here too – as any teenager with an MP3 collection of self-released music from unsigned artists can tell you – theory has been killed off by the facts. Whether you are Mick Jagger, or a great national artist from the third world looking for a global audience, or a garret-dweller reinventing music, the recording industry will soon have nothing to offer you that you can't get better for free. And music doesn't sound worse when distributed for free, pay what you want directly to the artist, and don't pay anything if you don't want to. Give it to your friends; they might like it.

Eben Moglen, 'Anarchism Triumphant: Free Software and the Death of Copyright', in Eli Lederman and Ron Shapira (eds), *Law, Information and Information Technology* (The Hague: Kluwer Law International, Law and Electronic Commerce Series, 2001), pp. 145, 170–1

Today's Legal Paradigm	Tomorrow's Legal Paradigm
Legal service	**Legal service**
One-to-one	One-to-many
Reactive service	Proactive service
Time-based billing	Commodity pricing
Restrictive	Empowering
Defensive	Pragmatic
Legal focus	Business focus
Legal process	**Legal process**
Legal problem-solving	Legal risk management
Dispute resolution	Dispute pre-emption
Publication of law	Promulgation of law
Dedicated legal profession	Legal specialists and information engineers
Print-based	IT-based legal systems

The role of law in a precarious world

As it unfolds, the 21st century yields few reasons to be cheerful. Our world continues to be blighted by war, genocide, poverty, disease, corruption, bigotry, and greed. More than one-sixth of its inhabitants – over a billion people – live on less than $1 a day. Over 800 million go to bed hungry every night, representing 14% of the world's population. The United Nations estimates that hunger claims the lives of about 25,000 people every day. The relationship between poverty and disease is unambiguous. In respect of HIV/AIDS, for example, 95% of cases occur in developing countries. Two-thirds of the 40 million people infected with HIV live in sub-Saharan Africa.

Amid these gloomy statistics, occasional shafts of light appear to justify optimism. There has been some progress in diminishing at least some of the inequality and injustice that afflict individuals and groups in many parts of the world. And this has been, in no small measure, an important achievement of the law. It is easy, and always fashionable, to disparage the law, and especially lawyers, for neglecting – or even aggravating – the world's misery. Yet such cynicism is increasingly unfounded in the light of the progress, albeit lumbering, in the legal recognition and protection of human rights.

The adoption by the United Nations, in the grim shadow of the Holocaust, of the Universal Declaration of Human Rights in 1948, and the International Covenants on Civil and Political Rights, and Economic, Social and Cultural Rights in 1976, demonstrates, even to the most sceptical observer, a commitment by the international community to the universal conception and protection of human rights. As mentioned above, this so-called International Bill of Rights, with its inevitably protean and slightly kaleidoscopic ideological character, reflects an extraordinary measure of cross-cultural consensus among nations.

The idea of human rights has passed through three generations. The first generation consisted of mostly 'negative' civil and political rights. A right is negative in the sense that it entails a right not to be interfered with in certain prohibited ways, for example my right to speak freely. A right is positive, on the other hand, when it expresses a claim to something such as education or health or legal representation. These second-generation rights crowd under the umbrella of economic, social, and cultural rights. The third generation of rights comprises primarily collective rights which are foreshadowed in Article 28 of the Universal Declaration which declares that 'everyone is entitled to a social and international order in which the rights set forth in this Declaration can be fully realized'. These 'solidarity' rights include the right to social and economic development and to participate in and benefit from the resources of the earth and space, scientific and technical information (which are especially important to the Third World), the right to a healthy environment, peace, and humanitarian disaster relief.

It is sometimes contended that unwarranted primacy is given to positive rights at the expense of negative rights. The latter, it is argued, are the 'genuine' human rights, since without food, water, and shelter, the former are a luxury. The reality, however, is that both sets of rights are equally important. Democratic governments that respect free speech are more likely to address the needs of the poor. And, on the other hand, in societies where economic and social rights are protected, democracy has an enhanced prospect of success since people are not preoccupied with concerns about their next meal.

Misgivings surrounding the concept of human rights are not new. Marxists, for example, have long rejected the very idea that the law can be a neutral body of rules which guarantees liberty and legality. They spurn, in short, the ideal of the rule of law. Others of a communitarian disposition dislike the individualism implicit in human rights. Qualms are expressed by those who perceive the expanding recognition of human rights as undermining the 'war on terror'. Still others find many of the rights expressed in declarations to be incoherent or cast in such vague and general terms, and weakened by inevitable exclusions and exemptions, that often they appear to take away with one hand what they give with the other. In impoverished countries, modern conceptions of human rights are at times regarded with suspicion as Western or Eurocentric, failing to address the problems of starvation, poverty, and suffering that afflict many of their people. Indeed, it is asserted that they merely shore up the prevailing distribution of wealth and power.

These, and many other, doubts about the development of human rights are not to be lightly dismissed. Nor should we be under any illusion that international, or indeed domestic, declarations or the agencies that exist to implement them are adequate. They provide the contours of a strategy for improved protection. The role of the numerous non-governmental organizations (NGOs), independent human rights commissions, pressure groups, and courageous individuals are of paramount importance. The growing body of law on the subject does promote a degree of optimism about the future well-being of humanity. In view of our planet's ecological

Law and the state

Modern law's strength is as a technical instrument of government, and as a medium of power. Legal ideas, as a framework of understanding of the character of social life, are moulded in numerous situations and processes of social interaction – in confrontations in the courtroom, negotiations in lawyers' offices, the regulation or containment of disputes in neighbourhood settings, the bargaining practices of regulatory agencies, the elaboration of police culture, and so on. Nevertheless, the character of law as institutionalized doctrine is most strongly shaped by coercive state power which stands in the shadows or sometimes clearly in view in all those settings where state law is invoked or impossible to avoid.

Roger Cotterrell, *The Sociology of Law: An Introduction*, 2nd edn (OUP, 1992), p. 312

despoliation and even potential nuclear immolation, it is necessary, if not essential, to conceive of rights as a weapon by which to safeguard the interests of all living things against harm, and to promote the circumstances under which they are able to flourish.

A fundamental shift in our social and economic systems and structures may be the only way in which to secure a sustainable future for our world and its inhabitants. The universal recognition of human rights seems to be an indispensable element in this process. The compelling rhetoric of the Marxist historian E. P. Thompson in defence of the rule of law rings equally true in respect of the universality of human rights:

> To deny or belittle this good is, in this dangerous century when the resources and pretensions of power continue to enlarge, a desperate error of intellectual abstraction. More than this, it is a self-fulfilling error, which encourages us to give up the struggle against bad laws and class bound procedures, and to disarm ourselves before power. It is to throw away a whole inheritance of struggle about law, and within the forms of law, whose continuity can never be fractured without bringing men and women into immediate danger.

This was written of the last century. These dangers have unquestionably intensified in this troubled century.

The future will doubtless challenge the capacity of the law not only to control domestic threats to security, but also to negotiate a rational approach to the menace of international terror. Public international law and the United Nations Charter will continue to offer the optimal touchstone by which to determine what constitutes tolerable conduct in respect of both war and peace. 'Humanitarian intervention' has in recent years become a significant feature of the international scene. Whether it be ethnic cleansing (Bosnia, Rwanda, Kosovo) or collapse of governments (Somalia and several sub-Saharan states), there is increasing support for action to prevent or avoid the horrors of such gruesome flashpoints. Moreover, in a world in which the law must confront an insidious enemy within, the very foundations of international law are severely tested. This war is waged not between states, but by a clandestine international terrorist network with pernicious ambitions.

It is easy, especially for lawyers, to exaggerate the significance of the law. Yet history teaches that the law is an essential force in facilitating human progress. This is no small achievement. Without law, as Thomas Hobbes famously declared,

> there is no place for Industry, because the fruit thereof is uncertain; and consequently no Culture of the Earth, no Navigation, nor use of the commodities that may be imported by sea; no commodious Building, no instruments of moving and removing such things as require much force; no Knowledge of the face of the Earth, no account of Time, no Arts, no Letters, no Society; and which is worst of all, continual fear and danger of violent death; and the life of people, solitary, poor, nasty, brutish, and short.

If we are to survive the calamities that await us, if civilized values and justice are to prevail and endure, law is surely indispensable.

References

Chapter 1

'[B]asic institutions, concepts, and values…': Harold J. Berman, *Law and Revolution: The Formation of the Western Legal Tradition* (Harvard University Press, 1995), p. 165.

'Like a jewel in a brooch…': H. R. Hahlo and Ellison Kahn, *The South African Legal System and Its Background* (Juta, 1968), p. 218.

Learned Hand, 'I often wonder…': *The Spirit of Liberty: Papers and Addresses of Learned Hand*, collected, and with an introduction and notes, by Irving Dilliard (Alfred A. Knopf, 1954), p. 190.

Alfred Denning, 'The Need for a New Equity', *Current Legal Problems* 1 (1952), 9.

H. L. A. Hart, The idea of 'justice consists of two parts': *The Concept of Law*, 2nd edn, ed. P. A. Bulloch and J. Raz (Clarendon Press, 1994), p. 156.

Jeremy Bentham, *An Introduction to the Principles of Morals and Legislation*, ed. J. H. Burns and H. L. A. Hart (Athlone Press, 1970) (*The Collected Works of Jeremy Bentham*, ed. J. H. Burns), Chapter 1, para 1.

Rupert Cross, 'Each and every pupil told me…': *Statutory Interpretation* (Butterworth, 1976), preface.

Bentham on 'dog law' and 'the more antique…': Quoted in Gerald J. Postema, *Bentham and the Common Law Tradition* (Clarendon Press, 1989), pp. 278–9.

Chapter 3

H. L. A. Hart, 'Positivism and the Separation of Law and Morals', *Harvard Law Review* 71 (1958), 593.

Lon L. Fuller, 'Positivism and Fidelity to Law – A Reply to Professor Hart', *Harvard Law Review* 71 (1958), 530.

Report of the Committee on Homosexual Offences and Prostitution, Chairman Sir John Wolfenden (Cmnd 247), Para 61.

John Stuart Mill, *On Liberty*, ed. Gertrude Himmelfarb (Penguin Books, 1974), pp. 72–3.

Patrick Devlin, *The Enforcement of Morals* (Oxford University Press, 1965), p. 14.

Ronald Dworkin, *Life's Dominion: An Argument about Abortion and Euthanasia* (HarperCollins, 1993), pp. 4 and 103.

United Kingdom, Abortion Act 1967, and Section 37 of the Human Fertilization and Embryology Act 1990.

Chapter 4

Edmond N. Cahn, *The Sense of Injustice* (Oxford University Press, 1949), p. 133.

Ronald Dworkin, *Taking Rights Seriously* (Duckworth, 1978).

Judith Resnick, 'Civil Processes', in Peter Cane and Mark Tushnet (eds), *The Oxford Handbook of Legal Studies* (Oxford University Press, 2005), p. 761.

Chapter 5

'Civil law jurisdictions recognize two categories of legal professionals...': Richard L. Abel and Philip S. C. Lewis, 'Lawyers in the Civil Law World', in Richard L. Abel and Philip S. C. Lewis (eds), *Lawyers in Society: The Civil Law World* (Beard Books, 2005), p. 4.

Chapter 6

Lawrence Lessig, *Code: Version 2.0* (Basic Books, 2006).

Free Software Foundation website: http://www.fsf.org

Table on page 148 adapted from Richard E. Susskind, *The Future of Law: Facing the Challenges of Information Technology*, revised edn (Clarendon Press, 1998).

Thomas Hobbes, *Leviathan*, ed. M. Oakeshott (Blackwell, 1960), chapter XIII.

Cases discussed

Chapter 2

Alcock v Chief Constable of South Yorkshire Police [1992] 1 A.C. 310.
(Football stadium case discussed on pages 45–6). The quote is
from Lord Hoffmann's speech at page 914.

*Associated Provincial Picture Houses Limited v Wednesbury
Corporation* [1948] 1 K.B. 223.

Carlill v Carbolic Smoke Ball Co. [1893] 1 Q.B. 256.

Donoghue v Stevenson [1932] A.C. 562 (H.L.) at 580 per Lord Atkin.
(The 'neighbour principle' quoted on pages 47–8.)

Hall v Brooklands Auto-Racing Club (1933) 1 K.B. 205. The 'man on
the Clapham omnibus' is first mentioned by Greer L.J.

MacPherson v Buick Motor Co. 111 N.E. 1050 (N.Y. 1916).

Rylands v Fletcher (188) L.R. 3 H.L. 330.

Stilk v Myrick (1809) 2 Camp. 317, 170 Eng. Rep. 1168 (Sailor case on
pages 41–2).

Chapter 3

Shaw v Director of Public Prosecutions [1962] A.C. 220 (H.L.) at 267,
per Lord Atkin.

Roe v Wade 410 U.S. 113 (1973).

Airedale NHS Trust v Bland [1993] A.C. 789 at 824–5 *per* Hoffmann
L.J. and at 859 *per* Mustill L.J.

Chapter 4

Marbury v Madison (1803) 5 US (1 Cranch) 137.

Chapter 5

Gideon v Wainwright, 372 U.S. 335 (1963).

Rondel v Worsley [1969] 1 A.C. 191 at 227 (per Lord Reid). The source of the quotation on the 'cab-rank' rule on pages 114–15.

Chapter 6

Brown v Board of Education of Topeka, 347 U.S. 483 (1954).

Cubby, Inc. v CompuServe Inc. 776 F. Supp. 135 (S.D.N.Y. 1991).

Stratton Oakmount v Prodigy 23 Med. L.R. 1794 (S.C., Nassau County 1995).

Godfrey v Demon [1999] EMLR 542 (English decision mentioned on page 146).

Legal sources: a very short explanation

When referring to an article in a legal journal or a decision of a court, I have included its recognized citation. This is standard practice, and, though I have kept such references to an absolute minimum, they are there in the hope that you might wish to peruse some of these sources in their complete and original form.

The method of citing legal journals or law reviews is fairly straightforward and requires no exposition here. The subject of case citations, on the other hand, is one of huge and complex proportions that would require a chapter-length elucidation. In any event, unlike lawyers and law students of my generation (who were obliged to search the shelves of dusty tomes in pursuit of an elusive law report), today's search engines provide instant Internet access to cases merely by keying in the names of the parties. There are, in addition, an assortment of databases which provide full text retrieval of cases, legislation, and law review articles. The best known (and probably the most comprehensive) are LexisNexis and Westlaw. Both contain an extensive selection of legal documents. A number of websites, many of them free, include www.bailii.org, www.lawreports.co.uk, www.europa. eu, www.echr.coe.int, www.worldlii.org, www.findlaw.com.

An excellent account of how to unearth the law is to be found in James A. Holland and Julian S. Webb, *Learning Legal Rules: A Student's*

Guide to Legal Method and Reasoning, 6th edn (Oxford University Press, 2006), Chapter 2.

In order to make sense of the references in this book, however, the following should suffice. Take the English case of *Donoghue v Stevenson* [1932] A.C. 562 (H.L.) mentioned on pages 47–8. In a civil decision such as this, the name of the case is normally dictated by those of the parties: Mrs Donoghue sued Mr Stevenson. The date in square brackets signifies that the year is an essential part of the reference. Round brackets indicate that the year is not of major importance, though it is included as a matter of course. 'A.C.' is an abbreviation of Appeal Cases, the name of the official report in which the decision appears. The number that follows is the page on which the case appears. '(H.L.)' is an abbreviation for the Judicial Committee of the House of Lords, which decided the case.

The approach is slightly different in the United States. For example, in the case of *Brown v Board of Education*, 347 U.S. 483 (1954) discussed on page 131, Brown is the plaintiff, the Board of Education, the defendant. The number 347 is the volume number of the reports in which the case appears. 'U.S.' is the abbreviation of *United States Reports*. The number 483 refers to the page on which the report begins, and 1954 is the year in which the judgment was delivered.

The system adopted in Europe and several other countries, as well as a detailed account of the major common law citation conventions, and those of other courts, such as the European Court of Human Rights, are admirably described in the following Wikipedia article: http://en.wikipedia.org/wiki/Case_citation.

Further reading

Chapter 1

John N. Adams and Roger Brownsword, *Understanding Law*, 4th edn (Sweet and Maxwell, 2006).

P. S. Atiyah, *Law and Modern Society*, 2nd edn (Oxford Paperbacks, 1995).

John Austin, *The Province of Jurisprudence Determined and the Uses of the Study of Jurisprudence* (Weidenfeld and Nicolson, 1954).

J. H. Baker, *An Introduction to English Legal History*, 4th edn (LexisNexis, 2002).

Manlio Bellomo, *The Common Legal Past of Europe, 1000–1800: 4 (Studies in Medieval and Early Modern Canon Law)*, tr. Lydia G. Cochrane (Catholic University of America Press, 1995).

Jeremy Bentham, *A Fragment on Government; or, A Comment on the Commentaries*, 2nd edn (W. Pickering, 1823).

Jeremy Bentham, *An Introduction to the Principles of Morals and Legislation*, ed. J. H. Burns and H. L. A. Hart (Athlone Press, 1970) (*The Collected Works of Jeremy Bentham*, ed. J. H. Burns).

Jeremy Bentham, *Of Laws in General*, ed. H. L. A. Hart (Athlone Press, 1970) (*The Collected Works of Jeremy Bentham*, ed. J. H. Burns).

Harold J. Berman, *Law and Revolution: The Formation of the Western Legal Tradition* (Harvard University Press, 1995).

G. L. Certoma, *The Italian Legal System* (Butterworth, 1985).

Albert H. Y. Chen, *An Introduction to the Legal System of the People's Republic of China* (Butterworths Law, Asia, 1992).

Guang Chen, Zhang Wang, Wang Chen Guang, and Zhang Xian Chu (eds), *Introduction to Chinese Law* (Sweet and Maxwell, Asia, 2001).

Richard Chisholm and Garth Nettheim, *Understanding Law: An Introduction to Australia's Legal System* (Lexis Law Publishing, 1992).

J. M. J. Chorus, *Introduction to Dutch Law*, 3rd edn (Kluwer Law International, 1998).

Andrew Clapham, *Human Rights: A Very Short Introduction* (Oxford University Press, 2007).

Council of Europe, *The Rebirth of Democracy: 12 Constitutions of Central and Eastern Europe* (Council of Europe, 1996).

François Dessemontet and Tugrul Ansay (eds), *Introduction to Swiss Law*, 3rd edn (Kluwer Law International, 2004).

Albert Venn Dicey, *Introduction to the Study of the Law of the Constitution*, ed. Roger E. Michener, 8th rev. edn (Liberty Fund, 1982).

Ronald Dworkin, *Taking Rights Seriously*, new impression with a reply to critics (Duckworth, 1978).

Ronald Dworkin, *A Matter of Principle* (Harvard University Press, 1985).

Ronald Dworkin, *Law's Empire* (Belknap Press, 1986).

Catherine Elliott, Carole Geirnaert, and Florence Houssais, *French Legal System and Legal Language* (Longman, 1998).

Catherine Elliott, Eric Jeanpierre, and Catherine Vernon, *French Legal System*, 2nd edn (Longman, 2006).

Emily Finch and Stefan Fafinski, *Legal Skills* (Oxford University Press, 2007).

George P. Fletcher and Steve Sheppard, *American Law in a Global Context: The Basics* (Oxford University Press, 2005).

Nigel Foster and Satish Sule, *The German Legal System and Laws*, 3rd edn (Oxford University Press, 2002).

Michael Freeman, *Human Rights: An Interdisciplinary Approach* (Polity Press, 2002).

Lawrence M. Friedman, *American Law in the Twentieth Century* (Yale University Press, 2002).

Lawrence M. Friedman, *American Law: An Introduction*, 2nd edn (W. W. Norton, 1999).

Lawrence M. Friedman and Rogelio Perez-Perdomo (eds), *Legal Culture in the Age of Globalization: Latin America and Latin Europe* (Stanford University Press, 2003).

Yash Ghai, *Hong Kong's New Constitutional Order: The Resumption of Chinese Sovereignty and the Basic Law*, 2nd edn (Hong Kong University Press, 1999).

Robert Gleave and Eugenia Kermeli (eds), *Islamic Law: Theory and Practice* (B. Tauris, 2001).

H. Patrick Glenn, *Legal Traditions of the World: Sustainable Diversity in Law* (Oxford University Press, 2007).

H. Patrick Glenn, *On Common Laws* (Oxford University Press, 2007).

Stephen Guest, *Ronald Dworkin*, 2nd edn (Edinburgh University Press, 1997).

H. R. Hahlo and Ellison Kahn, *The South African Legal System and Its Background* (Juta, 1968).

John Owen Haley, *The Spirit of Japanese Law* (University of Georgia Press, 2006).

Phil Harris, *Introduction to Law*, 7th edn (Cambridge University Press, 2007).

H. L. A. Hart, *The Concept of Law*, ed. P. A. Bulloch and J. Raz, 2nd edn (Clarendon Press, 1994).

Thomas Hobbes, *Leviathan*, ed. M. Oakeshott (Blackwell, 1960).

Tony Honoré, *About Law: An Introduction* (Oxford University Press, 1996).

K. D. Kerameus and P. J. Kozyris, *Introduction to Greek Law*, 2nd edn (Kluwer Law International, 1988).

Michael Lobban, *White Man's Justice: South African Political Trials in the Black Consciousness Era* (Clarendon Press, 1996).

Michael Loewe and Edward L. Shaughnessy (eds), *The Cambridge History of Ancient China: From the Origins of Civilization to 221 BC* (Cambridge University Press, 1999).

Stanley B. Lubman, *Bird in a Cage: Legal Reform in China after Mao* (Stanford University Press, 2002).

Chibli Mallat, *Introduction to Middle Eastern Law* (Oxford University Press, 2007).

Elizabeth Martin and Jonathan Law (eds), *A Dictionary of Law* (Oxford Paperback Reference, Oxford University Press, 2006).

Elena Merino-Blanco, *Spanish Law and Legal System*, 2nd edn (Sweet and Maxwell, 2005).

John Henry Merryman, *The Civil Law Tradition: Introduction to the Legal Systems of Western Europe and Latin America*, 2nd edn (Stanford University Press, 1969).

S. F. C. Milsom, *Historical Foundations of the Common Law*, 2nd edn (LexisNexis, 1981).

R. D. Mulholland, *Introduction to the New Zealand Legal System* (Butterworths Law, New Zealand, 1990).

Barry Nicholas, *An Introduction to Roman Law* (Clarendon Press, 1975).

Manfred Nowak, *Introduction to the International Human Rights Regime: No. 14* (Raoul Wallenberg Institute Series of Intergovernmental Human Rights Documentation, 2005).

Lester Bernhardt Orfield, *The Growth of Scandinavian Law* (Lawbook Exchange Ltd, 2002).

Vernon V. Palmer, *Mixed Jurisdictions Worldwide: The Third Legal Family* (Cambridge University Press, 2007).

Martin Partington, *Introduction to the English Legal System*, 3rd edn (Oxford University Press, 2006).

Amanda Perreau-Saussine and James B. Murphy (eds), *The Nature of Customary Law: Legal, Historical and Philosophical Perspectives* (Cambridge University Press, 2007).

Richard A. Posner, *Law and Legal Theory in England and America* (Clarendon Press, 1996).

Gerald J. Postema, *Bentham and the Common Law Tradition* (Clarendon Press, 1989).

Ravi Prakash, *The Constitution, Fundamental Rights and Judicial Activism in India* (Mangal Deep, India, 1998).

John Rawls, *A Theory of Justice* (Oxford University Press, 1973).

John Rawls, *Political Liberalism* (Columbia University Press, 1993).

Geoffrey Robertson, *Crimes Against Humanity: The Struggle for Global Justice* (Penguin Books, 2006).

Lawrence Rosen, *The Anthropology of Justice: Law as Culture in Islamic Society* (Cambridge University Press, 1989).

Malise Ruthven, *Islam: A Very Short Introduction* (Oxford University Press, 1997).

William A. Schabas, *An Introduction to the International Criminal Court*, 2nd edn (Cambridge University Press, 2004).

Brij Kishore Sharma, *Introduction to the Constitution of India* (Prentice-Hall, India, 2005).

Robert J. Sharpe and Kent Roach, *The Charter of Rights and Freedoms*, 3rd edn (Essentials of Canadian Law, Irwin Law, 2005).

A. W. B. Simpson, *Invitation to Law* (Blackwell, 1988).

Gary Slapper, *How the Law Works* (Collins, 2007).

Peter Stein, *Roman Law in European History* (Cambridge University Press, 1999).

Alexander Vereshchagin, *Judicial Law-Making in Post-Soviet Russia* (UCL Press, 2007).

Raymond Wacks (ed.), *The Future of the Law in Hong Kong* (Oxford University Press, China, 1991).

Raymond Wacks (ed.), *The New Legal Order in Hong Kong* (Hong Kong University Press, 1999).

Raymond Wacks, *Philosophy of Law: A Very Short Introduction* (Oxford University Press, 2006).

Raymond Wacks, *Understanding Jurisprudence: An Introduction to Legal Theory* (Oxford University Press, 2005).

Ian Ward, *A Critical Introduction to European Law*, 2nd edn (LexisNexis, 2003).

Thomas Wegerich and Anke Freckmann, *The German Legal System* (Sweet and Maxwell, 1999).

Peter Wesley-Smith, *An Introduction to the Hong Kong Legal System*, 3rd edn (Oxford University Press, China, 1999).

Glanville Williams and A. T. H. Smith, *Learning the Law*, 13th edn (Sweet and Maxwell, 2006).

Konrad Zweigert and Hein Kötz, *An Introduction to Comparative Law*, tr. Tony Weir (Clarendon Press, 1998).

Law

Chapter 2

P. P. Craig and Grainne de Burca, *EU Law*, 3rd edn (Oxford University Press, 2002).

Helen Fenwick and Gavin Phillipson, *Text, Cases and Materials: Public Law and Human Rights*, 2nd edn (Routledge Cavendish, 2003).

George P. Fletcher and Steve Sheppard, *American Law in a Global Context: The Basics* (Oxford University Press, 2005).

James A. Holland and Julian S. Webb, *Learning Legal Rules: A Student's Guide to Legal Method and Reasoning*, 6th edn (Oxford University Press, 2006).

Ian Loveland, *Constitutional Law, Administrative Law, and Human Rights: A Critical Introduction*, 4th edn (Oxford University Press, 2006).

Alastair Mowbray, *Cases and Materials on the European Convention on Human Rights*, 2nd edn (Oxford University Press, 2007).

Clare Ovey and Robin White, *Jacobs and White: European Convention on Human Rights*, 4th edn (Oxford University Press, 2006).

Ian Ward, *A Critical Introduction to European Law*, 2nd edn (LexisNexis, 2003).

Chapter 3

Thomas Aquinas, *Summa Theologiae*, in *Selected Political Writings*, tr. J. G. Dawson, ed. P. D'Entrèves (Blackwell, 1970; reprint of 1959 edn).

Aristotle, *Nichomachean Ethics*, tr. H. Rackham (Loeb Classical Library, Heineman, 1938).

Ronald Dworkin, *Life's Dominion: An Argument about Abortion and Euthanasia* (London: Harper Collins, 1993).

John Finnis, *Natural Law and Natural Rights* (Clarendon Press, 1980).

John Finnis, *Fundamentals of Ethics* (Georgetown University Press, 1983).

John Finnis (ed.), *Natural Law* (Dartmouth, 1991).

Lon Luvois Fuller, *The Morality of Law*, rev. edn (Yale University Press, 1969).

Robert P. George, *In Defense of Natural Law* (Oxford University Press, 1999).

Joseph Raz, *The Authority of Law: Essays on Law and Morality* (Clarendon Press, 1979).

Joseph Raz, *The Morality of Freedom* (Oxford University Press, 1986).

Joseph Raz, *Ethics in the Public Domain: Essays in the Morality of Law and Politics* (Clarendon Press, 1994).

Wojciech Sadurski (ed.), *Ethical Dimensions of Legal Theory* (Poznan Studies in the Philosophy of the Sciences and the Humanities, Rodopi, 1991).

Raymond Wacks, *Law, Morality, and the Private Domain* (Hong Kong University Press, 2001).

Chapter 4

Aharon Barak, *The Judge in a Democracy* (Princeton University Press, 2006).

Marcel Berlins and Clare Dyer, *The Law Machine*, 5th edn (Penguin Books, 2000).

Ronald Dworkin, *Justice in Robes* (Belknap Press, 2006).

Jeffrey Goldsworthy (ed.), *Interpreting Constitutions: A Comparative Study* (Oxford University Press, 2007).

J. A. G. Griffith, *The Politics of the Judiciary*, 5th edn (Fontana Press, 1997).

Carlo Guarnieri, Patrizia Pederzoli, and Cheryl Thomas, *The Power of Judges: A Comparative Study of Courts and Democracy* (Oxford University Press, 2002).

John Morison, Kieran McEvoy, and Gordon Anthony (eds), *Judges, Transition, and Human Rights* (Oxford University Press, 2007).

David Pannick, *Judges* (Oxford University Press, 1987).

William H. Rehnquist, *The Supreme Court* (Vintage Books USA, 2002).

Robert Stevens, *The English Judges: Their Role in the Changing Constitution* (Hart Publishing, 2005).

Chapter 5

Richard L. Abel, *American Lawyers* (Oxford University Press, 1991).

Richard L. Abel and Philip S. C. Lewis, 'Lawyers in the Civil Law World', in Richard L. Abel and Philip S. C. Lewis (eds), *Lawyers in Society: The Civil Law World* (Beard Books, 2005).

Richard L. Abel and Philip S. C.Lewis (eds), *Lawyers in Society: The Common Law World* (University of California Press, 1988).

Mary Jane Mossman, *The First Women Lawyers: A Comparative Study of Gender, Law and the Legal Professions* (Hart Publishing, 2006).

Stephen Nathanson, *What Lawyers Do: A Problem Solving Approach to Legal Practice* (Sweet and Maxwell, 1997).

David Pannick, *Advocates* (Oxford University Press, 1992).

Wilfrid R. Prest, *The Rise of the Barristers: A Social History of the English Bar, 1590–1640* (Clarendon Press, 1991).

Chapter 6

David Bainbridge, *Introduction to Computer Law*, 5th edn (Longman, 2004).

Colin J. Bennett, *Regulating Privacy: Data Protection and Public Policy in Europe and the United States* (Cornell University Press, 1992).

James Boyle, *Shamans, Software and Spleens: Law and the Construction of the Information Society* (Harvard University Press, 1997).

Roger Cotterrell, *The Sociology of Law: An Introduction* (Butterworths, 1984).

David DeGrazia, *Animal Rights: A Very Short Introduction* (Oxford University Press, 2002).

Lilian Edwards and Charlotte Waelde (eds), *Law and the Internet: A Framework for Electronic Commerce*, 2nd edn (Hart Publishing, 2004).

Andrew T. Kenyon and Megan Richardson (eds), *New Dimensions in Privacy Law: International and Comparative Perspectives* (Cambridge University Press, 2006).

Graeme Laurie, *Genetic Privacy: A Challenge to Medico-Legal Norms* (Cambridge University Press, 2002).

Lawrence Lessig, *Code: Version 2.0* (Basic Books, 2006).

Ian Lloyd, *Legal Aspects of the Information Society* (LexisNexis, 2000).

Ian Lloyd, *Information Technology Law*, 4th edn (LexisNexis, 2004).

Paul Przemyslaw Polanski (ed.), *Customary Law of the Internet: In the Search for a Supranational Cyberspace Law* (Asser Press, 2007).

Chris Reed, *Internet Law: Text and Materials*, 2nd edn (Cambridge University Press, 2004).

Chris Reed and John Angel (eds), *Computer Law: The Law and Regulation of Information Technology*, 6th edn (Oxford University Press, 2007).

Tom Regan, *The Case for Animal Rights* (University of California Press, 2004).

Jeffrey Rosen, *The Unwanted Gaze: The Destruction of Privacy in America* (Vintage Books, 2001).

Roger Scruton, *Animal Rights and Wrongs* (Continuum, 2006).

Peter Singer (ed.), *In Defense of Animals: The Second Wave*, 2nd edn (Blackwell, 2005).

Daniel J. Solove, *The Digital Person: Technology and Privacy in the Information Age* (New York University Press, 2006).

Cass R. Sunstein and Martha C. Nussbaum (eds), *Animal Rights: Current Debates and New Directions* (Oxford University Press, 2006).

Richard E. Susskind, *The Future of Law: Facing the Challenges of Information Technology* (Oxford University Press, 1998).

Richard E. Susskind, *Transforming the Law: Essays on Technology, Justice and the Legal Marketplace* (Oxford University Press, 2003).

Douglas Thomas and Brian Loader (eds), *Cybercrime: Law Enforcement, Security and Surveillance in the Information Age* (Routledge, 2000).

Raymond Wacks, *The Protection of Privacy* (Sweet and Maxwell, 1980).

Raymond Wacks, *Personal Information: Privacy and the Law* (Clarendon Press, 1989).

Raymond Wacks (ed.), *Privacy* (Dartmouth, 1993).

Raymond Wacks, *Privacy and Press Freedom* (Blackstone Press, 1995).

Raymond Wacks, *Law, Morality, and the Private Domain* (Hong Kong University Press, 2001).

Law

Index

Index

Law

U

W

Expand your collection of
VERY SHORT INTRODUCTIONS

ANARCHISM
A Very Short Introduction
Colin Ward

The word 'anarchism' tends to conjure up images of aggressive protest against government. But is anarchism inevitably linked with violent disorder? Do anarchists adhere to a coherent ideology? What exactly is anarchism?

In this Very Short Introduction, Colin Ward considers anarchism from a variety of perspectives: theoretical, historical, and international, and by exploring key anarchist thinkers from Kropotkin to Chomsky. Among the questions he ponders are: can anarchy ever function effectively as a political force? Is it more 'organized' and 'reasonable' than is currently perceived? Whatever the politics of the reader, Ward's argument ensures that anarchism will be much better understood after reading this book.

'excellent introduction' – **The Guardian**

http://www.oup.co.uk/isbn/0–19–280477–4

FREE WILL
A Very Short Introduction
Thomas Pink

Every day we seem to make and act upon all kinds of free choices – some of them trivial, and some so consequential that they may change the course of our life, or even the course of history. But are these choices *really* free? Or are we compelled to act the way we do by factors beyond our control? Is the feeling that we could have made different decisions just an illusion? And if our choices are not free, why should we be held morally responsible for our actions?

Thomas Pink, a leading authority on the subject, looks at a range of issues surrounding this fundamental philosophical question, exploring it from the ideas of the Greek and medieval philosophers through to the thoughts of present-day thinkers.

http://www.oup.co.uk/isbn/0–19–285358–9

PHILOSOPHY
A Very Short Introduction
Edward Craig

This lively and engaging book is the ideal introduction for anyone who has ever been puzzled by what philosophy is or what it is for.

Edward Craig argues that philosophy is not an activity from another planet: learning about it is just a matter of broadening and deepening what most of us do already. He shows that philosophy is no mere intellectual pastime: thinkers such as Plato, Buddhist writers, Descartes, Hobbes, Hume, Hegel, Darwin, Mill and de Beauvoir were responding to real needs and events – much of their work shapes our lives today, and many of their concerns are still ours.

'A vigorous and engaging introduction that speaks to the philosopher in everyone.'

John Cottingham, University of Reading

'addresses many of the central philosophical questions in an engaging and thought-provoking style ... Edward Craig is already famous as the editor of the best long work on philosophy (the Routledge Encyclopedia); now he deserves to become even better known as the author of one of the best short ones.'

Nigel Warburton, The Open University

www.oup.co.uk/isbn/0-19-285421-6

ANIMAL RIGHTS
A Very Short Introduction
David DeGrazia

Do animals have moral rights? If so, what does this mean?
What sorts of mental lives do animals have, and how
should we understand their welfare? After putting forward
answers to these questions, David DeGrazia explores the
implications for how we treat animals in connection with
our diet, zoos, and research.

> 'This is an ideal introduction to the topic. David DeGrazia
> does a superb job of bringing all the key issues together
> in a balanced way, in a volume that is both short and very
> readable.'
>
> **Peter Singer, Princeton University**

> 'Historically aware, philosophically sensitive, and with
> many well-chosen examples, this book would be hard to
> beat as a philosophical introduction to animal rights.'
>
> **Roger Crisp, Oxford University**

www.oup.co.uk/isbn/0-19-285360-0